CAN-DO

Creating self-directed, responsible, caring children

BY KATHY DOUGLAS

ILLUSTRATED BY GARY MOHRMAN

Totline® Publications
A Division of Frank Schaffer Publications, Inc.
Torrance, California

Managing Editor: Mina McMullin
Editor: Kathleen Cubley
Contributing Editors: Jean Warren, Kathy Zaun
Editorial Assistant: Mary Newmaster
Graphic Designer (Interior): Sarah Ness
Illustrator (Cover): Gary Mohrman
Production Manager: Janie Schmidt

ISBN: 1-57029-287-6

Printed in the United States of America
Published by Totline® Publications
23740 Hawthorne Blvd.
Torrance, CA 90505

INTRODUCTION

Each day, we have the opportunity to teach children positive values and to encourage them to be good citizens. *Can-Do Kids* is the perfect way to teach children four important values: responsibility, kindness, cooperation, and respect. It is filled with a wonderful variety of activities that promote these four basic values.

Four chapters, one for each value, are included in this book. Each chapter begins with tips for teaching the value and contains stimulating activities that span the curriculum. Many are designed to be done in groups, which encourage children to work together and get along. Each activity includes a materials list, easy-to-follow directions, and ideas for how to share. Often, ideas are provided to vary or extend it, too. By completing these activities, your children will also be developing such important skills as creative thinking, critical thinking, social-emotional, and gross and fine motor.

When you teach the four featured values in this book, children become aware of the importance of positive behavior in their day-to-day activities. This positive behavior leads to positive messages that will serve to motivate the children to use these values daily throughout their lives.

Kathy Douglas

CONTENTS

CONTENTS

KINDNESS

KINDNESS

With every interaction children have or observe, they learn about kindness. They learn to distinguish kind actions from unkind actions. Young children are innately kind, and it is our responsibility to protect and foster that natural innocence into an important lifelong value.

This chapter contains a wonderful variety of exciting activities the children can do to learn all about being kind—to themselves, to others, to other living things, and to property. They help the children learn that kindness is something we all need to live by every day.

People who work with young children are fortunate to be able to spread kindness all around. We are able to show children what kindness is and what it feels like. We can encourage kindness throughout the day through positive statements, through generosity, by integrating lessons and activities that promote kindness, and through caring for pets, plants, the environment, and people.

Through promoting kindness, we help children learn about helping others, giving, and using kind words. Teaching kindness as a value helps children grow into nurturing, warm, loving members of society.

TIPS FOR TEACHING KINDNESS

Kindness is a trait everyone needs. Below are some tips you should consider to help children learn about kindness.

- As teachers, we can build faith and trust by teaching and showing children how to be kind. We can let children know that their environment is a kind place.

- Since children model our behavior, treating them with kindness is one of the best ways to demonstrate kindness throughout the day.

- Kindness can be promoted by encouraging your children to use good manners at all times. Have your children use good manners when interacting with you, each other, classroom guests, and so on.

- Kindness is contagious, so pass it around. When you catch someone being kind, let everyone know it and watch how it spreads.

- Teach children to share by utilizing family-style eating—reinforce how we share food with each other by taking a serving and passing it to our friend.

- Show kindness in nonverbal ways—with smiles, hugs, laughter, and eye contact.

KINDNESS CHANT AND POSTER

Practice the Kindness Chant below with the children each day during circle time. Talk to them about the words in the chant and ask how those words make the children feel. Then have them create a kindness poster. The children can go to the language arts area throughout the day and tear or cut out pictures of things that make them feel good. Invite them to glue the pictures onto a sheet of posterboard or chart paper on which you have written the kindness chant.

Occasionally, take the kindness poster to circle time and discuss the pictures the children have selected. Ask the children why they picked certain pictures. Talk about being kind to ourselves, to others, and to the planet.

Materials

posterboard or chart paper

felt tip markers

magazines

scissors

glue

Preparation

Print the Kindness Chant below on posterboard or chart paper. Place the kindness poster in the language arts center, along with the magazines, scissors, and glue.

KINDNESS CHANT

Sharing, caring, and saying nice words
Are ways to be kind to each other.

Taking the time to give a smile,
Being there to give a hug—
Kindness is a wonderful thing.

Sprinkle kindness throughout the day
And see happy faces around you!

Kathy Douglas

Skills Used
Social/Emotional Skills
Critical Thinking Skills

Variation

Cut out large letter Ks and let the children glue pictures of people being kind onto the letters. Use the letter Ks on a "K Is for Kindness" display board.

THE GENTLE GARDEN

Talk to the children about how we should take care of plants. Tell them that we need to be gentle with them and say kind words to them. Plants are kind to us—they give us oxygen to breathe and beauty to see. During circle time, read a story or poem about tending flowers. Let the children look at a variety of different books about flowers.

Take the children outside to the pool planter (see Preparation below) and show them the potted flowers. Tell the children that they are going to plant a Gentle Garden. Discuss how the children need to take care of the flowers with kind, gentle hands. Give examples of ways to kindly and gently care for plants, such as gently touching the plants when necessary, talking quietly and kindly to the plants, and making sure the plants have just enough, but not too much, water. Encourage each child to dig a small hole in the soil. Show the children how to gently turn over the flowers, take them out of their pots, and gently place them in the soil. Have each child pat the soil around his or her flowers and then water and mist them.

Have the children visit their Gentle Garden each day and tend to the flowers. Encourage the children to take care of the garden by misting, watering, pruning, and saying kind words to the flowers.

Materials
awl or scissors, medium-size plastic swimming pool, two large bags of potting soil, variety of potted flowers, watering cans, misting bottles, books about gardens, story or rhymes about flowers

Preparation
Use an awl or a pair of sharp scissors to punch some small drainage holes in a medium-size plastic swimming pool. Set the pool in an outdoor area that is conducive to the sunlight needs of the flowers the children will plant. Fill the pool with potting soil. Fill watering cans and misting bottles and set them near the pool.

Variation
Plant a vegetable garden instead of a flower garden.

Skills Used
Social-Emotional Skills
Creative Thinking Skills

BEING KIND TO MYSELF

Talk to the children about how nice it is to take care of ourselves. Let them know that it is important and okay to take time to relax and enjoy the simple pleasures in life. Tell them that they are going to just relax for a few minutes. To help them relax, show them the "just for fun" materials (below). Invite the children to select things that make them feel good. Observe the choices they make.

After the relaxing activity, join together and ask the children how they feel. Encourage words such as relaxed, happy, rested, etc. The children may feel energized and ready to learn and play actively again. Let them know that this feeling is one of the benefits of being kind to themselves. Explain that when they are rested and relaxed, they will have more energy and be able to think more clearly than if they are tired or upset.

Materials

tablecloth, books, blankets, bubbles, drawing pads, crayons, paper, pencils, card games, and other "just for fun" activities or materials

Preparation

Set the materials out on a table or on a tablecloth on the ground.

Variation

Have the children lay on blankets outside and relax looking at clouds and trees.

Skills Used
Critical Thinking Skills
Motor Skills

KINDNESS BROWNIES

Gather a group of three or four children together. Help the children follow the directions on a box of ready-made brownie mix to make brownie batter. Encourage them to take turns adding the ingredients and stirring the mix. Tell the children that the brownies need a special secret ingredient in order to be truly yummy. Place the bowl in the center of the table and let everyone pretend to add the special ingredient. Invite them to sprinkle in lots of love, a handful of care, bunches of kindness, a dash of happiness, etc. Have the children put in as much kindness as they like. This is a wonderful opportunity for the children to use kind words. Bake the brownies and serve them with kindness and love.

Materials
ready-made brownie mix and ingredients needed to make the brownies

cooking utensils

mixing bowl

wooden spoons

pan

Preparation
Set the materials out on a table.

Variation
Instead of brownies, make kindness cookies using heart cookie cutters.

Skills Used
Social-Emotional Skills
Creative Thinking Skills

KINDNESS WISHING WANDS

Let each child make a wishing wand. Begin by having each child select a shape (see below). Have the children place stickers on their shapes. Show them how to tape a straw to the back of their shapes.

Talk to the children about kindness wishes. Tell them that kindness wishes are kind things they can do, or wish they could do, for people, animals, and plants. Have the children take their wishing wands and wave them around to make kindness wishes. Let them share their kindness and spread it all through the classroom and then go outside and make more wishes.

Materials

scissors
construction paper
sparkly stickers
plastic straws
tape

Preparation

From construction paper, cut out a variety of 3-inch wide shapes, such as hearts, stars, diamonds, and circles. Set out sparkly stickers, plastic straws, and tape.

Variation

Let the children "make" kindness dust. Let each child decorate a small paper bag. Tell them that the bags are full of kindness dust, and all they have to do is reach inside and pull out the kindness dust. Let the children spread the kindness dust all around.

Skills Used
Critical Thinking Skills
Motor Skills

NATURE'S KIND GIFTS

Let the children observe the different gifts from nature. Discuss how wonderful it is that nature gives us these kind gifts. Talk about why these items are gifts, using words such as beauty, fragrance, discovery.

Hold up each nature item and have the children name the item. Have them close their eyes while you remove one item from the tray. Ask the children to open their eyes to see if they can name the missing item. Repeat the game as long as interest lasts.

Materials

leaves, pine cones, flowers, water, bark, shells, stones, and other natural items that nature has been kind enough to give to us

Preparation

Display five to seven nature items on a tray.

Variation

To play a game of nature hide-and-seek, hide a variety of natural objects outdoors and let the children find them.

Skills Used
Critical Thinking Skills

KIND CARDS

Tell the children stories about being special and kind. Let them know how important it is to spread kindness around. Express to them that making cards for other people is a very nice way to tell people that they are special and to send them kind thoughts. Give the children the opportunity to make cards and give them to people who are special in their lives. They can make them for their friends, parents, teachers, and other people who are special. Another time, let the children draw names and make cards for each other.

Materials

construction paper	crayons
felt tip markers	stickers
rubber stamps	stamp pads

Preparation

Set out the materials in the language arts center. Fold a few pieces of construction paper into cards so the children will have some models.

Variation

Instead of cards, let the children make kindness posters for people.

Skills Used
Critical Thinking Skills
Creative Thinking Skills

KINDNESS SQUEEZE

Have all the children sit in a large circle indoors or outdoors. Begin by saying kind words about the children and about friendship. Talk about the specific ways you saw them spreading kindness around the area today. Tell the children that you know a special Kindness Squeeze that you're going to send to each of them. Gently squeeze the hand of one of the children sitting next to you and tell that child to gently squeeze the child's hand next to him or her. Have the children continue giving kind squeezes around the circle until the kindness gets back to you. Play the game again, this time singing the song below.

Materials
none

Preparation
none

KINDNESS ALL AROUND

Sung to: "London Bridge Is Falling Down"

Kind squeezes all around
All around, all around.
Kind squeezes all around
Around our circle.

Caring squeezes all around
All around, all around.
Caring squeezes all around
Around our circle.

Kathy Douglas

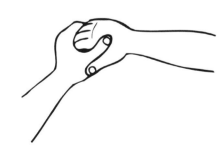

Variation
Instead of squeezes, pass a "kindness ball" around the circle.

Skills Used
Social-Emotional Skills
Critical Thinking Skills

HUG A TREE

Set up a simple puppet show about the wonder of trees. Include information about trees providing oxygen for us to breathe, homes for animals, and shade to keep us cool. Encourage the children to look at pictures of trees in the books.

Take a walk to an area with trees. Let the children hug the trees and thank them for being so kind to us. Have the children observe the trees to see if any of them are providing shade, homes for animals, or something beautiful for us to see.

Materials
puppets
books about trees

Preparation
Select a place to walk where the children can observe trees.

Variation
Encourage the children choose a tree to "adopt." Let them draw pictures of the tree, write stories about the tree, and observe the tree throughout the seasons.

Skills Used
Creative Thinking Skills
Critical Thinking Skills
Motor Skills

KIND ANIMAL PUPPETS

At circle time, discuss kindness with the children. Ask them what they think being kind means. Tell them stories that use examples of being kind. Most children will tell you being kind is sharing, not hitting, playing together, or being someone's friend. Reinforce these answers, and bring up other topics, such as being kind to animals. Ask the children how they are kind to animals and how animals are kind to them.

Have the children make animal puppets. Show the children how to use felt tip markers or crayons to draw animal faces on paper bags. Let them add yarn hair and yarn or pompon tails to their puppets. Encourage the children to put on puppet shows to demonstrate how animals can be kind to each other.

Materials

brown lunch bags
tissue paper
construction paper
markers
scissors

yarn
glue
crayons
fabric
magazines

Variation

Arrange for your children to do something kind for animals, such as making bird feeders.

Preparation

Set out the materials in the language arts center or the art center.

Skills Used
Creative Thinking Skills
Critical Thinking Skills
Social-Emotional Skills

SHARING FRUIT

Select two or three children to be the "sharing children." Ask them to pass out fruit to their classmates. Emphasize that by eating apple pieces, the children are sharing the fruit. Have them practice saying "please" and "thank you" during this activity.

Ask the children how it feels to share with each other and what it's like to be able to be the one who passes around the fruit to share with their friends.

Materials
apples

napkins

plates

Preparation
Cut the apples into small sections and place a few on each plate.

Variation
Take turns during the week sharing homemade treats that the children make at home.

Skills Used
Social-Emotional Skills
Motor Skills

IF YOU'RE KIND AND YOU KNOW IT

Practice singing the song below with your children. Let them do the movements as they sing the song.

Materials
none

Preparation
none

IF YOU'RE KIND AND YOU KNOW IT

Sung to: "If You're Happy and You Know It"

If you're kind and you know it, wear a smile,
If you're kind and you know it, wear a smile.
If you're kind and you know it, and you really want to show it,
If you're kind and you know it, wear a smile.

If you care and you know it, give a hug,
If you care and you know it, give a hug.
If you care and you know it, and you really want to show it,
If you care and you know it, give a hug.

If you share and you know it, dance around,
If you share and you know it, dance around.
If you share and you know it, and you really want to show it,
If you share and you know it, dance around.

If you're nice and you know it, shake someone's hand,
If you're nice and you know it, shake someone's hand.
If you're nice and you know it, and you really want to show it,
If your nice and you know it, shake someone's hand.

Kathy Douglas

Skills Used
Social-Emotional Skills
Motor Skills

WEATHER CELEBRATION

Each day, discuss the weather with the children. Talk about how the weather can be kind to us by providing the sun to keep us warm and to help plants and trees grow. Also talk about the benefits of rain and other kinds of weather.

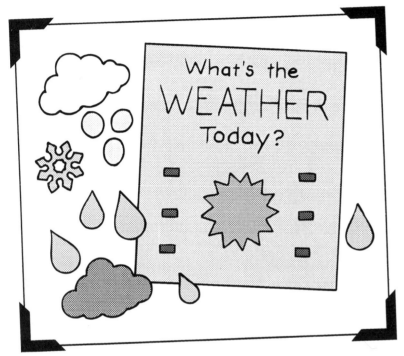

Discuss how weather is also sometimes unkind to us when hurricanes, floods, fires, or hail occurs. When it is too hot, plants, animals, and people struggle to be cool. Plants sometimes die because of too much heat. When it is too cold, plants freeze, and animals find it hard to stay warm. Discuss with the children what can happen when we don't have enough rain. Talk about what happens when we have too much rain or too little rain.

Each day, let the children observe the weather and place the appropriate symbols on the chart (see below) and predict the weather as they look out the window. Teach the children to be thankful for beautiful days, warm sunny skies, rainy days, and soft winds that blow seeds around.

Materials
posterboard
felt tip markers
self-stick Velcro
construction paper
scissors

Variation
On a rainy day, give each child a piece of construction paper. Invite them out into the rain and have them hold their papers out so raindrops can land on them. Let the children enjoy the different creations the raindrops make.

Preparation
From a variety of colors of construction paper, cut out different weather symbols, such as a sun, various sizes of raindrops, heavy rain cloud shapes, clouds, snowballs, snowflakes, and hail. You can even create wind signs. On a piece of posterboard, write "What's the Weather Today?" Place pieces from the soft side of a strip of Velcro on the backs of the weather symbols, and place pieces from the plastic side of the Velcro strip on the posterboard.

Skills Used
Critical Thinking Skills

TEACH THE WORLD TO SHARE

Practice singing the song below together. Let the children make up movements to the music.

Materials
none

Preparation
none

Variation
Spread kindness all around by singing the song to other groups in your school.

WE'D LIKE TO TEACH THE WORLD TO SHARE

Sung to: "I'd Like to Teach the World to Sing"

We'd like to teach the world to share
And be kind all the time.
We'd like to teach some love and care
And kindness everywhere.

We'd like to teach the world to be
A happy place to live.
We'd like to teach all people there
To be nice and to share.

We'd like to sing and dance all day
And spread kindness around.
We'd like to pass on all the love
And kindness we have found.

Kathy Douglas

Skills Used
Social-Emotional Skills
Motor Skills

LOST AND FOUND

During circle time, show the children pictures of items (or real items) that people might lose. Talk to the children about what happens when we lose something. How does it feel? What do we do when we lose something? Hold up an item or a picture and ask the children what they would do if they found the pictured item. Encourage the children to act with kindness when they find something that isn't theirs. For example, if they find a wallet at the store, they should tell their parents and ask them to take the wallet to the store manager. If they find something at school, they should give it to you. If they find something at the beach, they should take it to the lifeguard station. Think of other situations and let the children talk about what they would do.

Talk to the children about Lost and Found stations. Explain that many organizations have these stations where people can drop off found items. The people at the Lost and Found station keep the items until the people who lost the items come to find them.

Explain that lost children can also go to the Lost and Found station in stores and other places. The people at the station will use the loud speaker system to announce that a child is waiting for his or her parents at the station.

Materials

pictures of items (or real items) people might lose, such as keys, wallets, watches, and small toys

Preparation

Gather items you need.

Skills Used
Social-Emotional Skills
Critical Thinking Skills

Variation

Set out a Lost and Found box in your room. Let the children place found items in the box. Once a week (or as necessary), go through the box and ask what belongs to who. Be aware that children will probably put classroom items in the box. Take the opportunity to explain what types of things do and do not belong in the Lost and Found box.

SHOW AND SHARE

Gather the children together in a circle. Let each child take a turn talking about the item he or she brought to share (see page 26) for two or three minutes. Ask the child to pass the item around the circle so that everyone can have a chance to see and handle it. Let the children ask questions about the item. Talk about how kind it is to show interest in other people's things and ideas.

Taking turns at show and share time is often difficult for young children. Tell your children that part of sharing is letting everyone have a turn. You may want to set a timer for each child. Be sure to bring something to share yourself, and set the timer while you share.

Materials
none

Preparation
Photocopy the parent letter on page 26 and send one home with each of your children.

Variation
Have the children take turns bringing in a snack to share.

Skills Used
Critical Thinking Skills
Motor Skills

PARENT LETTER

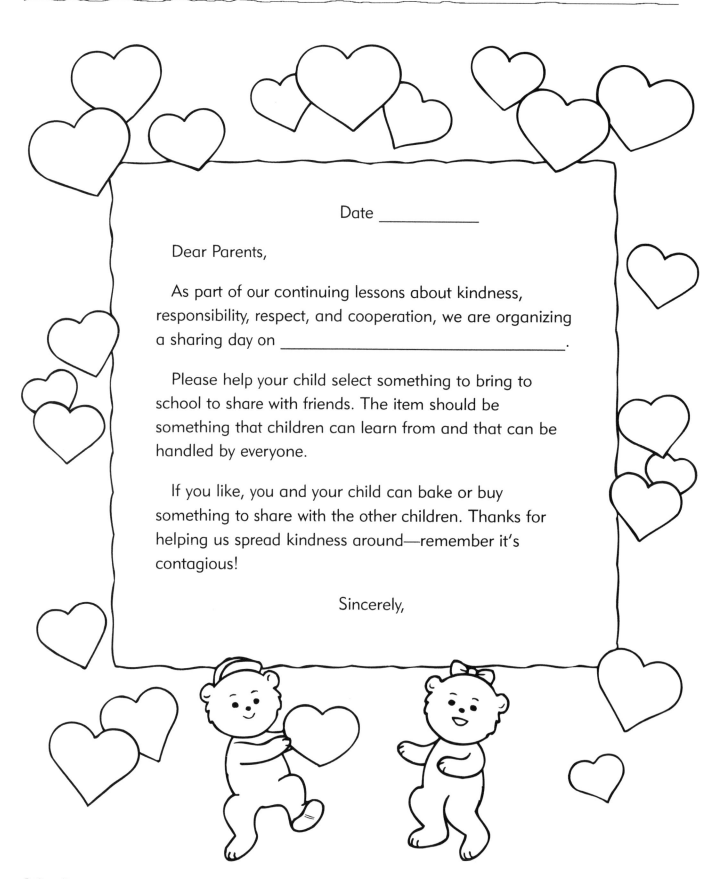

Date _____

Dear Parents,

As part of our continuing lessons about kindness, responsibility, respect, and cooperation, we are organizing a sharing day on _____.

Please help your child select something to bring to school to share with friends. The item should be something that children can learn from and that can be handled by everyone.

If you like, you and your child can bake or buy something to share with the other children. Thanks for helping us spread kindness around—remember it's contagious!

Sincerely,

THE KINDNESS RAINBOW

Talk to your children about what it means to be kind to one another. Let them know that during the week, you will be taking pictures of them when they are doing kind acts. The day you pick up the developed pictures, ask the children to help you paint a giant rainbow on a large piece of butcher paper. While you are all working together on the rainbow, talk about being nice, caring, sharing, and other acts of kindness. When the rainbow is dry, hang it on the wall at the children's eye-level. Let the children look through and enjoy the pictures of kind actions. Invite them to turn the rainbow into a Kindness Rainbow by attaching their pictures to it.

Take a picture of the children in front of the Kindness Rainbow and place it on the cover of a drawing tablet in the language arts center. Encourage the children to dictate stories or draw pictures about the kind actions shown on the Kindness Rainbow.

Materials

camera
paint
paintbrushes
crayons

film
smocks
butcher paper

Variation

Make a collage of people doing acts of kindness from magazine cuttings.

Preparation

Set out the materials in the art center.

Skills Used
Social-Emotional Skills
Creative Thinking Skills
Motor Skills
Critical Thinking Skills

VETERINARIAN'S CLINIC

At storytime, read the children a story about taking a pet to the veterinarian's clinic. After storytime, let them look through some basic pet care books. Take the children into the housekeeping area and show them the materials you have set out. Encourage the children to set up a veterinarian clinic. Be available to answer questions or provide reference material as needed.

Let the children take a lot of time for this activity. Encourage them to take turns playing veterinarian and pet owner. The children may want to pretend they are the animals, too. Talk about the acts of kindness veterinarians do every time they see a patient. As the children role-play, you may want to model taking care of pets at the clinic with them.

Demonstrate acts of caring and kindness to them. Let them know how important it is to take care of our pets. Explain that part of this care involves taking them to the veterinarian for check-ups and immunizations and caring for them when they are sick.

Materials

storybook about a visit to the veterinarian

pet care books

stuffed animals

toy doctors kits

note pads

toy telephones

pet food and water bowls

Variation

Set up a hospital in the dramatic play center.

Preparation

Place the materials in your housekeeping area.

Skills Used
Social-Emotional Skills
Motor Skills
Critical Thinking Skills

THE THINK BOX

Gather the children and ask them to sit in a circle with you. Show them the pillowcase (see below). Let the children take turns reaching in and pulling out an object. Ask them to name the object, and then have them tell you how they could use the object to be kind. They may pull out an umbrella and tell how they would share it with a friend on a rainy day. They may suggest inviting a friend to look at a storybook with them, or sharing a snack with someone.

Materials
pillowcase

construction paper

glue

scissors

various helpful items (umbrella, jacket, hat, toy food, books, toys)

Preparation
Place the objects in the pillowcase.

Variation
Instead of using real items in a pillowcase, find pictures of helpful items and place them in a box.

Skills Used
Critical Thinking Skills
Motor Skills
Social-Emotional Skills

THROW THAT BALL

Invite a group of three or four children to play ball with you. Before you begin, talk about being kind to each other by letting each person have a turn "making a basket." Explain that in this game, each child's turn lasts until he or she throws the ball into the basket. Then it is the next child's turn. Model encouraging statements for the children and ask them to join in. For example, "Great toss, Jason!" or "Good job!"

Materials
basket
rubber balls

Preparation
Set the basket and the balls in an area appropriate for ball play.

Variation
Play Duck, Duck, Goose.

Skills Used
Social-Emotional Skills
Motor Skills

KINDNESS OR SHARING?

Divide the children into two groups. Tell them you are going to take turns asking each group a question, and they should call out the answer if they know it. Each question is going to be about either an act of kindness or an act of sharing. (Sample questions are below.) Let the group that answered the most questions correctly pass out cookies for everyone to share.

Materials
cookies

Preparation
none

Examples
Below are examples of questions to get you started.

- What are you doing when you have two cookies and you give one to a friend? (sharing)

- What are you being when you give someone who's crying a hug? (kind)

- What are you doing when you break your cookie in half and give one of the halves to a friend? (sharing)

- What are you being when you gently pet a cat or dog? (kind)

- What are you doing when you offer to let your sister or brother play with one of your toys? (sharing)

Variation
Dramatize an act of kindness or sharing. Let the children tell you what it is.

Skills Used
Critical Thinking Skills
Motor Skills

THE LAND OF KINDNESS

Tell your children a make-believe story about a very special place where people live. Your story might begin, Once upon a time, in a far away land, lived many kind people who cared about each other and shared with each other. They said kind words and enjoyed working and playing together.

Insert your children's names into the story as you go along. For example, "One day, Molly was painting with Meg, and she wanted to do something kind, so she shared her yellow paint with Meg." Let your children tell parts of the story, too.

Materials
none

Preparation
none

Variation
Tell other stories with the children to teach other values. Let them create a book with you about the different tales.

Skills Used
Creative Thinking Skills
Critical Thinking Skills

THE FLOWER SHOP

During circle time, talk about the reasons people give flowers to each other—to express love, care, sympathy, well wishes, friendship, etc.

Show the children the materials in the housekeeping center (see below) and encourage them to set up a flower shop. Be available to help the children as needed. Let them know that the flower shop will stay "open" during the week, and they can make flower arrangements and cards to give as an act of kindness to different people. Let them know how wonderful it is to receive and give flowers to people.

Materials
real and artificial flowers, plastic vases, construction paper, markers, crayons

Preparation
Set all of the materials in the housekeeping center.

Variation
Bake cookies to take to an elder care facility.

Skills Used
Social-Emotional Skills
Creative Thinking Skills
Motor Skills
Critical Thinking Skills

FRIENDSHIP PUPPETS

Encourage the children to work in small groups and talk about making friends as they create paper-sack puppets. Have the children create one or two puppets. Let them glue symbols onto their puppets that reflect their feelings about friends. For example, if they choose to glue on a heart, they can talk about love. If they glue on smiley faces, they can discuss how friends make them happy.

Have the children work together to put on a small group puppet show. They can cooperatively decide how they will put on a small puppet show about friends in the language center or for many of their classmates.

Materials

scissors

yarn pieces

brown or white paper bags

crayons

glue

scraps of fabric and paper

Variation

Have the children make puppets to show ways families can be kind to each other.

Preparation

Set all of the materials out in the art center.

Skills Used
Creative Thinking Skills
Social-Emotional Skills

PROPAGATING KINDNESS

Talk to the children about plant growth and how nice it is to care for plants and share them. Show the children how to take a cutting from a plant. Select a healthy stem, cut it off, and set it on a tray. Select a bottle and fill it with water. Place the end of the plant in the water and set it back on the tray.

Each day, let the children mist the plant cuttings and check to make sure the stem is under water. In five to ten days, the cutting should sprout roots. At this point, it is time for planting.

Let the children plant the cuttings in small plastic pots. Help them tie a ribbon around each pot and send the plants home with the children as gifts.

Materials

plants that you can take cuttings from

water bottles or clear soda bottles

watering can

scissors

plastic trays

potting soil

plastic pots

ribbon

Preparation

Set up a propagation area in your science center. Place a few different plants around that are easily propagated, such as ivy, coleus, or spider plants. Place plastic bottles, a filled watering can, and scissors nearby.

Skills Used
Creative Thinking Skills
Social-Emotional Skills

RESPECT

RESPECT

Respect is such an important value. Being respectful means being considerate, paying attention to others, being good, sharing ideas, understanding others' feelings, and being honest. Teaching young children to respect themselves, other people, property, and all other living creatures is a value that will be carried forth with them forever.

This chapter is full of activities designed to teach children respect in a hands-on, interactive fashion. They help the children learn respect by doing.

Always remember that you are an important role model for the children. As a teacher and a facilitator, you will have the opportunity to encourage respect.

TIPS FOR TEACHING RESPECT

Since respect is such a valued character trait, be sure to read through the important tips below to help you teach children this valuable trait.

- Children learn respect through promoting and modeling. These are the best means to use to help children take care of toys and materials in their classroom environment.

- Teach your children to respect the outdoor environment by showing them where the garbage can is and telling them how very important it is to throw trash in the garbage can. Teach your children about recyclable materials. Set out boxes where the children can put recyclable paper, aluminum cans, plastic bottles, etc.

- Show children respect by communicating with them using non-restrictive language. For example, if the children can't go outdoors one day, explain this to them in clear terms they will understand. For example, "We can not go outside because the carpenters are fixing our playhouse, and they have lots of tools that we could get hurt with."

- Teach children to respect themselves by helping them learn to communicate their needs. Always respond to them in a developmentally appropriate manner.

THE LAND OF RESPECT

Talk with a small group of children about living together in a community that values respecting each other and the neighborhood. Discuss with the children why it is so important to respect your friends and neighbors in the community.

Have the children work together in a sandbox to build a neighborhood that represents living together respectfully. For example, encourage them to create their own sand houses and then have them develop the roads and waterways. Encourage the children to build parks and other community spaces.

While the children are napping, put pieces of trash in their community. When they look at their community, they will experience disrespect. Encourage a discussion about how they feel about the mess. They can discuss the rights of other people and what they could do to stop people from dumping trash in their community. Ideas include posting "no littering" signs and setting out paper-cup garbage cans on each block.

Materials

sandbox	sand toys
toy boats	toy cars
toy people	paper
markers	paper cups

Preparation
Set materials outside next to the sandbox.

Variation
Build a Land of Disrespect so children can see the opposite effect.

Skills Used
Social-Emotional Skills
Critical Thinking Skills

CARING FOR OUR TOYS

Discuss caring for toys with the children. Demonstrate proper care through role-play, showing the children how we can show respect and disrespect for toys. Let the children take turns dramatizing both respecting and disrespecting toys.

Have the children identify some of the objects that belong in the housekeeping center (see below). Let each child select an object from the housekeeping center. Set out a bucket of soapy water and give each of the children a rag. Have the children clean the objects.

Talk to the children about the condition of the objects they are handling. Are any of the items damaged? If so, what types of repairs are needed? Ask the children if they can work together to fix the objects. Tell them they can also recommend that you fix the objects or have them fixed by someone else. Talk about why the toys are broken. Are they simply old, or have they been mishandled? When the children are through with the activity, have them put all of the objects back where they belong.

Materials
dishes
dolls
table
chairs
dress-up clothing
rags
bucket of soapy water

Variation
Do the same activity in the block or art center.

Preparation
Set the materials out in the housekeeping center.

Skills Used
Critical Thinking Skills
Social-Emotional Skills

TAKING CARE OF ME COLLAGES

Discuss with the children how important it is to respect themselves. Let them know that they take care of themselves by bathing, washing their hair, getting dressed in clean clothing, combing their hair, brushing their teeth, and eating healthful foods. Ask the children questions about what other things they can do to respect their bodies, such as exercising and being safe.

When the discussion is finished, encourage each child to make a Taking Care of Me collage. Have the children cut out pictures from magazines and advertisements of objects that represent caring for themselves.

When the children are finished, ask them to tell you how they take of themselves. Write down the children's responses on the backs of their collages.

Materials
scissors

magazines

glue

construction paper

Preparation
Set out materials in the art center.

Variation
Show children how to take care of their fingernails, hair, and teeth by doing special demonstrations.

Skills Used
Social-Emotional Skills
Critical Thinking Skills

LISTENING TO EACH OTHER

Teaching children to listen to each other and to their teachers is very important. By playing the Listening to Each Other game, the children can learn to respect each other and show respect for their teachers.

Have the children sit in a large circle. Pick two names out of the stack of index cards (see below) and show them to the children. Have the two children whose names appear on the card stand in the middle of the circle. Ask each child to say something nice to each other. Next, have the other children tell you what they said. You can also play the game by picking a card from the stack and having the child tell you his or her favorite color, animal, or other interesting fact.

Materials
pen   index cards

Preparation
Print each child's name on an index card.

Skills Used
Social-Emotional Skills
Critical Thinking Skills

TEACHER RESPECT

With the help of the children, demonstrate appropriate and inappropriate ways to treat teachers. Try some of the following ideas: ask a child to pretend to give you flowers, have a child offer to help with a classroom task, ask a child to say "no" when you ask him or her to do something, or have a child pretend to break a classroom rule.

After each demonstration, have the children tell you whether to hold up (see below) the smiling face (for appropriate behavior) or the frowning face (for inappropriate behavior).

Materials
markers

paper plates

scissors

Variation
Have the children help you demonstrate appropriate and inappropriate behavior toward parents and toward each other.

Preparation
For each child, draw a smiling face on a paper plate and a frowning face on another paper plate.

Skills Used
Critical Thinking Skills
Social-Emotional Skills

RESPECTING OUR OCEANS

Select one of the picture books (see below). Gather a small group of children. Look at the book with them and discuss how wonderful our oceans are. Express to them how very important it is to respect the oceans by keeping them clean. Ask them what they can do to help keep the oceans clean.

Have the children sort through the materials and classify them into groups, such as shells, rocks, driftwood, and garbage. After they have classified the materials, ask them about each group and how these materials may have gotten into the ocean. Let them determine if the materials belong in the ocean or if people need to be more careful.

Materials

seashells

small rocks

driftwood

trash

picture books about the ocean

Variation

From magazines, cut out pictures of fish, boats, bottles, tires, and other objects that may or may not belong in the ocean. Have the children sort the pictures into two groups—*things that belong in the ocean* and *things that don't*.

Preparation

Set out the materials.

Skills Used
Critical Thinking Skills
Motor Skills

TAKING CARE OF THINGS

Give the children a chance to look at the toys on the tray (see below). Discuss with them how special these toys are to their owners. Explain how important it is to take care of toys and other things that belong to other people. Talk to them about respecting their things and other people's things. Show the children how to handle the toys. Pass the toys around for the children to hold and manipulate. Ask them what happens when we take care of our things and other people's things. What happens when we don't take care of these things?

Set out paper, scissors, and glue, along with some magazines. Let the children make a collage of things they would like to take care of in a respectful manner. Let them tell you how they would take care of these objects and treat them with respect.

Materials

toys belonging to the children

paper

scissors

glue

magazines

tray

Preparation

Place special toys out on the tray.

Skills Used
Critical Thinking Skills
Motor Skills
Social-Emotional Skills

MANNERS PUPPETS

Gather the children in a circle. Using two puppets, put on a puppet show about manners. Tell a story about one of the puppets using good manners and one of the puppets using poor manners. Have the puppets ask the children which manners are appropriate and which are inappropriate.

Next, let the children go to the puppet-making area and create manner puppets. When they have finished creating their puppets, encourage them to put on a puppet show for the other children.

Materials
markers

paper sacks

two puppets

stories that teach manners

Preparation
Set out a paper sack for each child. On each sack, print a manners word, such as *please, thank you, pardon me, excuse me, May I?,* etc.

Variation
Sit down and eat cookies and practice using manners.

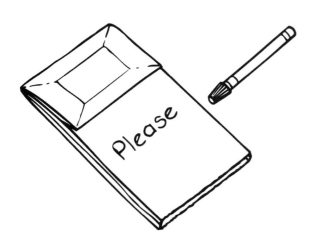

Skills Used
Critical Thinking Skills
Social-Emotional Skills

SHOPPING CONSIDERATION

Let the children take turns playing grocery store. Have them select different roles to play, such as bagger, checkout clerk, shoppers, etc. Demonstrate with the children how we show respect to people who help us in the grocery store and how they show respect to the shoppers. Also show children how some people show disrespect at the store. Let the children tell you how it feels to be respected and disrespected.

Encourage the children to play and enjoy the roles of teaching respect and interacting with each other as responsible citizens.

Materials
dramatic play materials for grocery shopping, such as a cash register, play food, baskets for groceries, etc.

Preparation
Set up the dramatic play area as a grocery store.

Variation
Go on a field trip to the grocery store. Look for people showing respect.

Skills Used
Social–Emotional Skills
Motor Skills

RESPECTING SAFETY RULES

Go over four or five safety rules you want your children to follow. Talk to them about how important it is to respect the rules. Give examples of following the rules. Have the children demonstrate how we follow the rules, and let them tell you what happens when we don't follow them.

Play Red Light, Green Light with the children, using red and green construction paper for the traffic lights. You can also let the children practice crossing the street safely by setting up a road and crosswalk using blocks and masking tape.

Create other safety rule games with the children, teaching such things as wearing seat belts and riding the school bus safely.

Materials
chart paper   markers

Preparation
On chart paper, print four or five safety rules that you want your children to follow.

Our Safety Rules
1. Wear Safety Belts.
2. Hold Your Partner's Hand
3. Look Both Ways Before
4. Don't Run With Scissors.

Skills Used
Critical Thinking Skills
Motor Skills

BIRDS NEED RESPECT

Take a small group of children into the bird station (see below). Let them look at the bird pictures and books about birds. Discuss with the children important facts about birds. Let them look at the food that birds eat and then have them observe the bird feeder. As the birds come to the feeder, ask the children questions such as these: "Do the birds feed alone or in a group? Do the birds feed on the ground or in trees? How do the birds act at the feeder? How many birds come to the feeder?"

When all the children in the class have completed the bird study, take them for a walk to see if they can find birdhouses, nests, or feeding areas. Tell the children about how and where birds build nests.

Let them know that it is important not to disturb birds in their nests, because if we handle the eggs or baby birds, the bird parents will not take care of them anymore.

Materials

pictures of birds, picture books about birds, bird food, bird feeder, bag of rice, red food coloring, other items toxic to birds

Variation

Call the Audubon Society for more information. Arrange for a guest speaker.

Preparation

Set up a bird station in the classroom. Hang pictures of birds, set out picture books about birds, and place bird food and other items out in the station. Place a bird feeder outside where the children can observe the birds.

Skills Used
Critical Thinking Skills

SAVE THE MANATEE CLUB

Teach your children to respect wildlife by introducing them to the endangered manatee. Read them a story and show them pictures of manatees. Have the children create manatee puppets with paper bags, pipe cleaners, and crayons. Let the children put on a puppet show about saving them.

Explain to the children how important it is to help save the manatees. Let them know that careless boaters, canal locks, barges, crab traps, discarded fishing line, and habitat destruction are some of the reasons manatees are endangered. If you are further interested, adopt a manatee by calling 800-423-JOIN or call (407) 539-0990.

Materials
pictures of manatees
books about manatees
crayons
paper bags
pipe cleaners
tape
information on how to join the Save the Manatee Club

Variation
Find out more information about other endangered animals.

Preparation
Set up a manatee station. Hang pictures of manatees and place picture books about manatees in the station. Set out paper, crayons, paper bags, pipe cleaners, and tape.

Skills Used
Motor Skills
Creative Thinking Skills

THE SIGN SAYS

Talk to the children about the different signs they see each day in their neighborhood. Show them the different signs you have and see if they can identify them and tell you what each sign means. Let them know that when we do what the signs say, it shows respect for following the rules. These rules are there to keep us safe from harm.

Have the children play a game with the different signs. For example, let the children take turns practicing walking across a crosswalk. You can make a crosswalk outside with chalk, or use masking tape to create an inside crosswalk. Play a stop and go game with a stop sign and tricycles. Put stop signs up in the designated tricycle area. You can also make miniature signs for the children to use in the block center.

Materials
construction paper

markers

pictures of signs from magazines

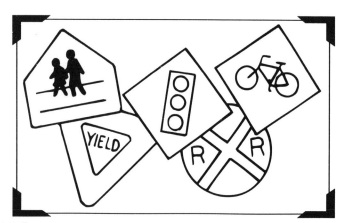

Preparation
On construction paper, draw such signs as *stop, walk/don't walk, no swimming, no trespassing, do not enter,* etc.

Variation
Go for a walk in the surrounding neighborhood and let the children identify different signs.

Skills Used
Social-Emotional Skills
Creative Thinking Skills
Motor Skills

PARDON ME

Have the children practice what to do when they need to say something to an adult who is speaking to another adult or child. Let them practice by role-playing different scenarios. For example, select three children and ask them to speak to each other about playing a game or choosing a center. Walk up to the children and say, "Excuse me, Johnny. I need to speak with you."

Another scenario may involve a teacher and a child talking. Have another child walk up to the teacher and say, "Excuse me, Ms. Smith, I need your help." There are many other situations that require a child to interrupt a conversation. Think of those that happen most in your classroom and set up different scenarios for the children to learn from.

You can also have the children practice patience by not interrupting when what they have to say could wait a minute or two.

Materials
none

Preparation
none

Variation
Put on puppet shows with the children that teach them how to say *excuse me* and *pardon me*.

Skills Used
Motor Skills
Critical Thinking Skills

COMMUNITY MUSIC

Introduce the instruments to the children (see below). Show them how to handle the instruments and treat them with respect. Let the children explore and experiment with the instruments. Have them talk about the instruments they are playing and say the names of the instruments. If you have community members who will come in and share music or sing, introduce them to the children and let them share their talents.

Listen to music from the community and give the children the opportunity to identify different instrumental sounds. Let the children move to the music and then talk about enjoying a wide variety of different types of music. This is a wonderful opportunity for the children to learn about and appreciate other people's musical preferences.

Materials
music from different cultures
instruments from different cultures

Preparation
Set out different instruments and find music that represents different cultures.

Variation
Have musicians come in and show the children their instruments. Teach them to respect the instruments and enjoy them.

Skills Used
Creative Thinking Skills
Social-Emotional Skills

WE ALL LIVE TOGETHER

Sit with the children and look through the various books with them (see below). Let the children point out things that are the same and different about the towns and cities. Talk about the people in the stories and how they are alike and how they are different.

Discuss how important it is to get along and show respect for each other by being good citizens. Ask the children what they must do to be good citizens. They might talk about being polite to each other, picking up litter, waving to community helpers, following safety rules, etc.

Have the children put on a puppet show about living in the community together. Through puppetry and daily interactions in the classroom, model for the children how we can all live together.

Materials
people puppets
books about towns and cities

Preparation
Set out the puppets and books in an area where a small group of children can work together.

Variation
Have the children go for a walk in the community and look for signs of respect.

Skills Used
Critical Thinking Skills
Social-Emotional Skills

RESPECTFUL ROLE-PLAYING

Dramatize different situations with the children and have them show you how they would act respectfully in each instance.

* *A child is at a swimming pool and has just finished eating a bag of chips. What should he or she do with the empty bag?*

* *A shopper at the grocery store drops a box of crackers. What should the child do?*

* *A child's father is cooking dinner and needs help setting the table. The child is playing in the living room. What should the child do?*

* *A child's mother is in the backyard and needs help picking up leaves. What should the child do?*

Materials

a variety of different props

Preparation

Select role-playing situations from those listed above (or make up your own). Gather the necessary materials.

Variation

Make up different situations and let the children dramatize them with puppets.

Skills Used
Creative Thinking Skills
Critical Thinking Skills

MY NAME IS . . .

Divide the children into small groups. Let the groups take turns going on a name hunt (see below). When they find their names, have them come back to the writing center and practice printing their names. Let each child draw pictures around his or her name. When the children have finished, let them bring their name cards to the area you have designated. Encourage them to talk about how important it is to have a name and for people to call you by your name.

Tell the children that when we call each other by name, it is very respectful. When we talk to adults, we call them Mr., Ms., or Mrs. to show respect. Ask the children to name some of the people they call Mr., Ms., or Mrs.

Materials

paper

index cards

crayons or pencils

markers

Preparation

Set out paper and crayons or pencils in the language arts center. Print the children's names on index cards and hang them around the classroom.

Variation

Make up a name song.

Skills Used
Social-Emotional Skills
Creative Thinking Skills

THE THREE BEARS

Talk to the children about what it means to be respectful to people, their possessions, the community, and the earth. Read the story (see below) to them slowly, discussing the different events that happen. Ask the children what they think about Goldilocks and how she treated the bears' house. For example, was it respectful for Goldilocks to just walk into the bears' house? Discuss all the things she did and talk about how the children would feel if someone did that to their houses. Let the children make up different endings to the story that will help Goldilocks be more respectful.

Materials
the book *Goldilocks and the Three Bears*

Preparation
Review the story and pick out the events that show respect and disrespect.

Variation
Read other stories to the children that involve respect.

Skills Used
Creative Thinking Skills
Critical Thinking Skills

GIVE ME SPACE

Talk to the children about respecting personal space. Let them know that it's okay to have space parameters. Then divide the children into groups of three. Give each child a sheet of paper you have prepared and have him or her step inside the circle (see below). Have them put on smocks and then move their papers wherever they want, as long as they don't touch any of the other children's papers in their group. Have the children look at the space they each have. Pass out paint and paintbrushes. Let the children enjoy painting their personal space.

Materials

scissors, butcher paper, smocks, paint, paintbrushes, small trays to hold paint

Variation

Give children their nap blankets and let them spread the blankets out to determine their space.

Preparation

Cut out a 4-by-3-foot piece of paper for each child. Cut a hole in the center of each piece of paper, large enough for a child to sit in. Lay the papers outside or in the art area. Place smocks near the paper and set out paint and paintbrushes.

Skills Used
Social-Emotional Skills
Creative Thinking Skills

PRIVACY PLEASE

Talk to the children about privacy in the restroom, including having respect for each other and taking turns when using the restroom. Ask them questions about why they need to respect each other's privacy while using the restroom. Ask the children what they can do to let each other know they are in the restroom.

Show them the red and green sign you have made (see below). Let them know that the green side means the restroom is empty, and the red side means the restroom is in use. Hang the sign on the restroom doorknob. Encourage the children to change the colors accordingly. Practice throughout the day for the first week and continue to remind them when necessary.

Restroom

Materials
scissors

red and green construction paper

yarn

markers

Preparation
Cut two large circles out of construction paper, one green and one red. Glue them together, back to back. Attach a loop of yarn to the circle.

Skills Used
Critical Thinking Skills

PLAYGROUND COLLAGES

Talk to the children about cleaning up after themselves outdoors. Let them know it shows respect for the people who are taking care of them and respect for themselves. Show the children the pictures (see below) and ask how they help clean up in the specific areas of the playground.

Take the children out on the playground and let them clean up any trash they see. When they are through, talk about what they found and ways they can keep the playground clean in the future.

Give each child a piece of construction paper, some pictures, scissors, and glue. Let the children make collages out of the playground pictures.

Materials

scissors

glue

construction paper

pictures of children playing outside and using playground equipment (school supply catalogs and family magazines are good sources for these pictures)

Preparation

Cut out the pictures and mount them on construction paper.

Skills Used
Social-Emotional Skills
Motor Skills
Critical Thinking Skills

GOTCHA!

Teach the children to use respectful words, such as please and thank you. "Catch" them using good manners throughout the day. Each time you hear a child using good manners, give this child a Happy Gram.

Materials
Happy Grams
small basket

Preparation
Make several photocopies of the Happy Gram. Cut them out and place them in a basket.

Variation
Hand out Happy Grams when you notice children doing acts of kindness.

HAPPY GRAM
Congratulations!
You have been caught being respectful.

Skills Used
Social-Emotional Skills

HUNTING FOR RESPECT

Take the children outside and let them hunt for things that show signs of respect. Some things they might look for are safety signs, garbage cans, people saying please and thank you, buildings that are taken care of, and parents taking care of their children.

Let the children hunt for signs of disrespect, such as garbage on the ground, broken windows, people speeding, broken playground equipment, etc. Talk with the children about the things they found on the treasure hunt.

After the hunt, let the children draw pictures of what they found while walking around the community. Hang the pictures up in the classroom.

Materials
paper, crayons, tape

Preparation
none

Variation
Have the children show respect for community helpers by making thank-you cards for firefighters, police officers, the school librarian, and others they might wish to thank.

Skills Used
Motor Skills
Critical Thinking Skills
Social-Emotional Skills

CATCH ME IF YOU CAN! BRACELETS

During circle time, go over the list of classroom rules with the children (see below). Have them recite the rules to you. Talk about why it is important to follow the rules. Give each child a construction paper bracelet to wear. Let them know that throughout the day, you will be playing Catch Me if You Can. Tell the children that when you "catch" them showing respect for the rules, you will place a sticker on their bracelets.

At different times during the day, have the children come together and count how many stickers they each have.

Materials

marker

chart paper

scissors

construction paper

tape

stickers

ruler

Variation

"Catch" the children being responsible, kind, or cooperative.

Preparation

Print the classroom rules on the chart paper and draw a symbol next to each rule. Keep the rules simple and positive. Hang the chart in a place so that all the children can see it. Cut a 1½-by-6-inch strip of construction paper for each child. Make the strips into bracelets by forming them into loops and taping the ends.

Skills Used
Critical Thinking Skills
Social-Emotional Skills

MY BOOKS, MY BOOKS

Gather a small group of children into the book area in your classroom. Talk to them about how wonderful it is to enjoy books. Show them hardback and softback books and discuss how to respect books by taking good care of them.

Ask the children how they respect and take care of their books. They might talk about turning the pages carefully, placing the books on shelves after reading them, and washing their hands before enjoying a book.

Show them a book in poor condition to demonstrate what happens to books that aren't taken care of. Let the children look through the books and practice book respect.

Materials
hardback and softback books

books in poor condition

Preparation
Set out a wide variety of good quality books for the children to use.

Variation
Set up a book hospital in your room. Place books that need repairs in an area with materials the children may use to fix them.

Skills Used
Critical Thinking Skills

FRIENDLY PICTURES

Let the children draw pictures of their friends. Have them select their skin color, eye color, and hair color. Talk about how we treat our friends with respect by being kind to them, sharing, saying please and thank you, and by laughing and having fun together.

As the children are drawing, play music or sing a song.

Materials
crayons (including skin tone crayons)
construction paper

Variation
Use paint and large sheets of paper and have the children paint life-size pictures of their friends.

Preparation
Set out the materials in the art area.

Skills Used
Motor Skills
Creative Thinking Skills
Social-Emotional Skills

RESPECTING OUR PETS

Read a story about pets to your children. Talk about the story and about what the children can do to show respect for the critters that live in their neighborhood.

Show them pictures of the animals and then take a walk around the neighborhood looking for pets. When you get back from the walk, have the children draw pictures of the animals they saw. Remember that even scribbled pictures of animals are symbols created by the children. Ask the children about their pictures. On the back of the pictures, write down their descriptions.

Materials

stories about pets

pictures of pets

construction paper

crayons

Preparation

Set the materials out in the art area.

Variation

Arrange for a guest speaker from a pet store or animal shelter to come talk to the children. You might also ask parents to bring in their well-mannered pets.

Skills Used
Motor Skills
Critical Thinking Skills

RESPONSIBILITY

RESPONSIBILITY

Responsibility is an important lifelong value, and preschool is the perfect time to begin reinforcing responsible behavior. Preschool children have many daily classroom responsibilities, such as cleaning up after themselves, taking care of pets, watering plants, being in charge of turning lights off when necessary, helping at snacktime, etc. They are also responsible for taking charge of their self-care activities, such as hand-washing, tooth-brushing, and feeding themselves. Children should also be required to manage and be responsible for their actions towards others and themselves.

Children learn responsibility from teachers, parents, friends, and community members. Teaching responsibility in the classroom and encouraging its growth promotes healthy development of the children in your care.

Using the hands-on activities in this chapter and modeling, you can foster responsibility in the classroom, on the playground, in the snack area, and at home. Providing children with the tools to be responsible is a gift that will open doors for each young child as he or she goes through life.

TIPS FOR TEACHING RESPONSIBILITY

Learning to be responsible is a big and important job for children. You can best help them by keeping the tips below in mind.

- Use the words *trustworthy, reliable, and accountable* several times each day. Encourage your children to use the words as well.

- Create an atmosphere of responsibility by encouraging children to be responsible. You can do this by giving each child a task or job to do during the week. For example, let two of the children be responsible for watering plants or feeding the classroom pets.

- Let your children be responsible for hanging up their own artwork. Facilitate this by setting out tape.

- Teach responsibility in the bathroom. Have a couple of children check the bathroom for trash, soap, and toilet paper. Older children can help stock the bathroom when supplies run low.

- Teaching children to take responsibility for their own actions is important. If a child is angry and acts inappropriately, let that child tell you what happened and write it down. Read it back to the child and have the child help you determine what should happen next to solve the problem.

CLASSROOM RESPONSIBILITIES

During circle time, discuss the different responsibilities children and teachers have when taking care of the classroom. As the children tell you the different responsibilities, write them down on chart paper.

Go over each responsibility with the children and ask them open-ended questions about them. Show them the responsibility cards (see below). On another sheet of chart paper, write down a child's name and then have that child pick a responsibility card. Tape the card onto the paper. Each day at circle time, discuss each child's responsibility task for the week. For bigger jobs, set up shared responsibilities by assigning two to four children to work cooperatively on a specific task, such as washing the tables.

Materials

felt tip markers
index cards
chart paper
tape
laminating material if available

Variation

Have the children make responsibility charts to hang in the classroom. You can also encourage the parents to make a responsibility chart for home.

Preparation

Write each of your classroom responsibilities on a separate index card. Cut out or draw a symbol to glue onto each card that represents the responsibility. For example, if one of the cards is for watering plants, cut out or draw a watering can and flowers. The picture will assist the children in identifying what they are responsible for that week or day.

Skills Used
Motor Skills
Critical Thinking Skills

PAPER FILING

Invite the children into the language arts center. Have them use the paper and writing utensils to make creations, such as pictures of their family and friends, cards, or books. Encourage or help each child print his or her name on the creation. When the children are finished, have them find the file folder (see below) with their name on it and place their work in the folder. These folders can be moved to other centers throughout the week so the children can file their work. Using the filing system will help the children learn to be responsible for putting their work and creations where they belong.

Materials

file folders	felt tip markers
cardboard box	paper
crayons	pencils

Variation

Make a "Family Connection" file box in which the children can place all correspondence that needs to go home to their families. Print a different child's name on each of the correspondence letters and set them on a table. Let the children take turns finding their letters and then filing them in their folders. It may be helpful to place the letters in two or three stacks for the children to take turns looking through.

Preparation

Write each child's name in large letters on a file folder. Place the files in a cardboard box. Place paper, felt tip markers, and crayons in the language arts center.

Skills Used
Motor Skills
Critical Thinking Skills

PLAYGROUND SAFETY INSPECTORS

During circle time, discuss the reasons why the children should play safely and use the equipment safely on the playground. Have the children tell you various playground safety rules. List the rules on a piece of chart paper as they state them. Go over the rules and talk to the children about being responsible when it comes to playground safety.

Talk about the equipment on the playground. Have the children go on a playground safety check with you and look for nails, lose boards, broken toys, and other items that may need repair.

When everyone has finished looking, sit down together and make a list of what needs to be repaired and what needs to be thrown away. Encourage the children to check frequently for playground hazards and to be responsible by following the playground safety rules.

Materials
markers

chart paper

Preparation
none

Variation
Have a playground beautification day. Discuss the environment and how we can all pitch in and help keep the planet clean. Then tell the children that you are all going to start keeping the planet clean right here on your playground. Give each child a paper garbage sack and lead the children outdoors to pick up garbage and other things that don't belong on the playground.

Skills Used
Motor Skills
Critical Thinking Skills

ARTISTIC RESPONSIBILITY

Place the chart (see below) in your art center. Invite your children to the art center. Be sure there are enough smocks to go around. Go over the chart with the children. Encourage their creative growth and their responsible actions towards materials.

Materials

felt tip markers   chart paper

art materials   smocks

sponges

Preparation

On chart paper, write out rules about using the art materials. Use rules such as wearing smocks, keeping art materials in the child's space, cleaning materials when through, putting the materials away, and hanging up smocks. Make the chart easily understandable to your children by using pictures and simple words.

Variation

Write responsibility charts for different centers in your room.

Skills Used
Critical Thinking Skills
Social-Emotional Skills

BEING A GOOD CITIZEN

After the guest (see below) tells the children about the organization and what they can do to help, have them create an "I Can Help" list. Ask the children how they think they can help, and write the ideas on a piece of chart paper. Let the children decide how they can help. Write down their answers on a sheet of chart paper and hang them up in your room.

Have the children create posters that reflect the needs of the organization. Encourage them to draw pictures, tear pictures from magazines, paint pictures, use rubber stamps or stickers, etc. Set aside an area in the classroom to display the group posters.

Write a note to the parents in your group explaining the organization, your children's involvement, and a list of some items that are needed. Place a collection box in your room to collect the items the children and parents donate to the organization.

Materials

felt tip markers
posterboard
paint
rubber stamps

chart paper
magazines
paintbrushes
stickers

Variation

To help animals, contact the Humane Society.

Preparation

Select an organization that helps people in need, such as the American Red Cross, United Way, Goodwill, or another organization in your community. Call the organization and ask how your group can get involved. Arrange for a guest speaker to come in and share information about the organization.

Skills Used
Critical Thinking Skills
Social-Emotional Skills

GOOD FOR YOU FOODS

Explain to the children who enter the center that there are many food choices that we make each day. Encourage them to look at the reference books (see below) and food choice charts. Ask them to select pictures of foods that they think are healthy choices. What foods help their bodies grow? Have them glue their healthy food choices onto a piece of paper. Encourage them to print their names on the papers or assist them. Hang the healthy food pictures in the science center. When time permits, have the children sit with you in small groups and discuss their food choices.

Materials

pictures of foods that are both good for you and not so good for you

food magazines

supermarket advertising fliers

construction paper

posterboard

glue

markers

scissors

books about food and nutrition

Variation

Let the children sort real foods into two groups: "healthy" and "not so healthy." Set out candy bars, cookies, soda pop, bread, cheese sticks, apples, etc.

Preparation

Cut out a wide variety of pictures of both healthy and not so healthy foods. Create two food choice charts. On one piece of posterboard, print "Healthy Foods." On the other piece of posterboard, print "Not So Healthy Foods." The children can glue pictures of foods on both charts. Place the sample charts in the science center along with the food pictures, construction paper, glue, and markers. Set out several books about food and nutrition as well.

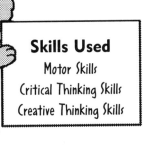

Skills Used

Motor Skills

Critical Thinking Skills

Creative Thinking Skills

HERB FUN

During circle time, discuss herbs with the children. Ask them what they think herbs need to grow healthy and strong (sunlight, water, misting, pruning, etc.). Tell the children the name of each herb and let them practice saying it. Write the name of each herb on an index card and set the appropriate card in front of each plant.

Explain to the children that we use these herbs to cook with, and that we eat them in a variety of foods. In small groups, let the children look at the herbs and mist them (let each child in the group take a turn misting one herb with one spray of the misting bottle). Have the children take turns cutting small pieces off different plants and tasting them. Teach the children to take care of the herbs in a responsible manner by checking the moisture of the soil using their fingers, misting the herbs a little each day, and pruning off dead leaves. Teach the children what the right moisture level is by watering one of the herbs so it is just right and letting the children feel the soil. Let the children know that if the soil is wetter than the example they felt, the plants do not need any more water for a day or so. Tell the children that following all of the guidelines discussed makes them responsible, caring gardeners.

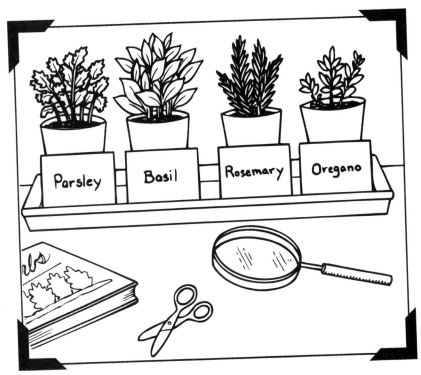

Materials

variety of herb plants

watering can

books on growing herbs

magnifying glass

misting bottle

plastic trays

scissors

Variation

Set up a window garden in the classroom and let the children tend it. Plant more herbs or fast-blooming flowers, such as marigolds or bachelor's buttons.

Preparation

Set a variety of herb plants on a plastic tray in a sunny place in the classroom. Place a watering can, a misting bottle, a magnifying glass, and a pair of scissors next to the herbs.

Skills Used
Motor Skills
Critical Thinking Skills
Social-Emotional Skills

FRESH, WONDERFUL AIR

On a sunny day, take your children outside and have them sit in a circle on the grass or a blanket. Talk about the beautiful weather. Encourage the children to take deep breaths. Discuss how good it feels to take deep breaths of fresh air. Talk about exercise and why it is important to stretch, walk, run, dance, skip, etc., for a little while each day. Talk about how good it feels to exercise and how exercise can be lots of fun.

Have everyone stand up, and then show your children some simple stretching exercises, such as reaching up high and bending low and touching toes. Then go for a nice brisk walk or jog. After doing some exercise, have the children get back into a circle and discuss how it felt to stretch, walk, and breathe in all that fresh air. Let your children know that taking care of their bodies through exercise and nutrition is part of being a responsible person.

Materials
none

Preparation
none

Variation
Set up a simple obstacle course on the playground and let the children take turns going through the course.

Skills Used
Motor Skills
Critical Thinking Skills

TOOTH-BRUSHING EXPERIENCE

Let your children look at the different types of toothbrushes (see below) and feel the bristles with their fingers. Ask them if they think the brushes are soft or hard. Let the children explore the contour of the handles on the brushes and measure them with a ruler. Have the children squeeze small amounts of toothpaste onto a paper plate and let them smell and touch each type of toothpaste. Ask them to choose their favorite toothbrush and toothpaste. Encourage the children to practice brushing seashells with their favorite toothbrush and toothpaste. Talk with the children about the responsibility of taking care of their teeth. Show them how to brush the shells up and down and side to side. Set a timer for 30 seconds and have the children brush their shells until the timer goes off. Tell them that this is how long they should brush their own teeth in the morning and at night. Have them show responsible behavior by rinsing the toothbrushes off and putting all of the items back in their proper place.

Materials

a variety of toothbrushes and tubes of toothpaste, cup, mirror, dental floss, information on caring for teeth, ruler, large seashells

Variation

Ask a dentist to donate enough toothbrushes so that each child can practice brushing his or her own teeth instead of using the shell.

Preparation

On a table, set out a variety of toothbrushes and tubes of toothpaste, a cup, a mirror, two or three containers of dental floss, a ruler, and several large seashells. Include pamphlets about caring for teeth (appropriate materials are available from pediatric dentists).

Skills Used
Motor Skills
Critical Thinking Skills

POURING MILK AND JUICE

Show the children how to open and close the milk cartons (see below) and pour water into a cup. Let the children take turns practicing pouring the water into cups. If they spill some of the water, encourage them to clean up their spill with paper towels. After the children have mastered this skill, let them try to pour their own juice or milk at snack time. Encourage the children to use their manners, saying such things as "Please pass the milk," and "Thank you." The children will not only become more responsible, but also more independent.

Materials
cups
empty pint-size milk cartons
paper towels
plastic tray

Preparation
In the math center, set out two to four cups, two to four empty pint-size milk cartons filled with water, and a plastic tray. Place paper towels out alongside the cups.

Variation
In the math center, let the children practice pouring rice or water into different sized measuring cups.

Skills Used
Motor Skills

PET RESPONSIBILITY

Encourage the children to observe and talk to the classroom pet or pets daily (see below). Discuss with them the reasons why it is so important to talk to and take care of pets. What would happen if they didn't take care of their pet?

During circle time, ask the children to brainstorm the tasks involved in taking care of their pet(s). List these tasks on a piece of chart paper, and then ask for volunteers to be responsible for each task. Write the children's names beside each task, followed by a row of boxes representing each day of one week. Place the chart near the pet area and let the children check off their task after it is completed each day. Always reinforce hand washing after taking care of the animals.

Our Pet		Mon	Tues	Wed	Thu	Fri
WATER	Mikaela	✓				
FOOD	Jerome					
TALK	Leo					
PLAY	Evvy					
CLEAN	Aggy					

Materials

classroom pet, pet food, water, plastic bowls, small pitcher, pet care reference books, felt tip markers, chart paper

Variation

Encourage your children to lend a hand to outdoor critters by setting up a bird feeder and keeping it stocked with birdseed.

Preparation

Set up the pet area by putting small amounts of food in a plastic bowl and placing water in a small pitcher beside a water bowl (or appropriate water container for the pet). Display pet care reference books around the pet area.

Skills Used
Motor Skills
Critical Thinking Skills
Social-Emotional Skills

BIKE HELMETS

Talk to the children about bike helmet safety. Discuss being responsible by wearing a helmet whenever they ride a tricycle or bicycle. Ask them different questions about what might happen if they ride a bike without a helmet. Show the children how to put on a bike helmet, and let each child have a turn to do so.

Ask each child to choose a piece of paper from the numbered pieces (see below). Have them tear or cut out enough bike or trike pictures to equal the number on their paper. Then have them tear or cut out the same number of bike helmets. (Pictures of bikes, trikes, and helmets are available in outdoor magazines, bike gear catalogs, store advertising fliers, etc.) Let the children glue the bikes and trikes onto their papers, and glue the helmets next to the bikes.

Materials

pictures of tricycles, bicycles, and bike helmets

a real bike helmet

glue

paper

markers

scissors

Variation

Create a simple matching game where the children draw lines between matching colored trikes and helmets.

Preparation

In the math center, set out variety of pictures of tricycles, bicycles, and bike helmets, a real bike helmet, glue, 10 pieces of paper, markers, and scissors. On each piece of paper, print a numeral from 1 to10, depending on the developmental range of the children in your group.

Skills Used
Motor Skills
Creative Thinking Skills
Critical Thinking Skills

SETTING THE TABLE

Talk to the children about how important it is to take turns setting the table for breakfast, lunch, or snack. Explain that we should wash our hands before handling the table setting materials. Let a small group of children set the table for breakfast, lunch, or snack. Show the children how to arrange the table setting, using the sample as their guide. Arrange a table setting group for each meal you serve throughout the day.

Materials

plates	cups
plastic forks and spoons	napkins
felt tip marker	posterboard

Preparation

Near the snack table, set out napkins, cups, plates, and plastic forks and spoons. On a piece of posterboard, arrange a place setting and trace around all of the pieces. Place this sample near the table.

Variation

Have the children arrange their own table settings and make name cards for themselves.

Skills Used
Motor Skills
Critical Thinking Skills

THIS IS THE WAY WE WASH OUR HANDS

Talk to the children about how important it is to wash our hands before eating and after going to the bathroom. Discuss why we need to be responsible by turning off the water to help conserve it.

Talk with your children about the steps they need to follow in order to make sure their hands are clean. Be sure to mention all of the steps below.

1. Turn on water and wet hands.

2. Turn off water.

3. Squirt soap onto hands.

4. Rub hands and make soapy bubbles.

5. Turn water back on and rinse hands.

6. Turn off water.

7. Dry hands and throw away the paper towels.

Throughout the day, have the children demonstrate the hand washing technique, one or two at a time.

Materials
paper towels, liquid soap, sink

Extension
Discuss other ways to conserve water, such as turning water off when brushing teeth and making sure faucets are turned all the way off each time.

Preparation
Make sure the paper towels and soap are stocked at the sink where your children wash their hands.

Skills Used
Social-Emotional Skills
Critical Thinking Skills

RESPONSIBILITY COLLAGE

Ask your children what they are responsible for during their morning routines. Ask them about getting dressed, eating breakfast, brushing hair and teeth, etc. Have the children tear or cut out pictures of some of the things they do in the morning to get ready for school.

Let the children make collages using the pictures. Help them print their names on their collages. Hang them up in your language arts center.

Have the children describe the different pictures they selected and tell you about their daily school responsibilities.

Materials
magazines
glue
scissors
construction paper

Variation
Have the children cut out and glue pictures of what they do to get ready for bed.

Preparation
Set out the materials in the language arts center.

Skills Used
Critical Thinking Skills
Creative Thinking Skills
Social-Emotional Skills

THE GARDENING PROJECT

Divide your children into four groups. Each group will tend a garden plot. Have each group make a name sign together for its flower garden. Give each group a packet of seeds. Show them how to sprinkle the seeds in little rows. Give each child a few seeds to plant, and let the children mist the soil. Teach the children how to check the soil for moisture by touching it with their fingers. Each day, let them check the soil and mist if necessary.

Materials

plastic tub filled with dirt

fast-growing seeds, such as marigolds or bachelor's buttons

misting bottles

four long sticks

Preparation

Use sticks to divide a plastic tub filled with dirt into four sections. Set out seeds and misting bottles.

Variation

Plant an outside garden in a large plastic pool. Be sure to poke holes in the bottom for drainage.

Skills Used
Social–Emotional Skills
Critical Thinking Skills

LOOK BOTH WAYS BEFORE YOU CROSS THE STREET

Discuss the importance of learning how to cross the street. Demonstrate this through role-play. Have the children put cars and people on the masking tape road (see below). Let the children use the toys to demonstrate how to safely cross the street. Encourage them to play and keep practicing safe street crossing.

Materials

blocks   action figures

toy cars   masking tape

Preparation

In the block center, use masking tape to make a road on the floor. Set out blocks, toy cars, and some of the children's action figures.

Variation

For older preschoolers getting ready to start kindergarten, practice school bus safety.

Skills Used

Social-Emotional Skills

Critical Thinking Skills

LET'S PLAY

Tell a story or have a discussion about being responsible by cleaning up after ourselves at home and in the classroom. Dramatize these actions with your children. Discuss the various ways the children can clean up at home and in the classroom. Encourage small groups of children to dramatize clean-up activities.

Have the children play in the dramatic play center in small groups. Encourage the children to clean up and role-play different household situations.

Materials
none

Preparation
none

Variation
Set up a grocery store and let the children practice the responsibilities of being a grocery employee.

Skills Used
Social-Emotional Skills
Creative Thinking Skills

RECYCLING FUN

Discuss why recycling is so important in helping the planet and how it is our responsibility to recycle and reuse whenever we can. Talk to your children about how they can help recycle at school and at home. Show them different types of recyclable materials (newspaper, cardboard, regular paper, etc.). Tell the children that it is important to sort these materials for the recycling workers.

Divide the children into small groups of two to four. Let one group at a time sort the recyclable and non-recyclable materials into separate piles. Then let the children sort the piles into some of the smaller categories you discussed earlier. When they are finished, encourage the children to place the materials back in the box for the next group to sort. Leave the activity in the science center and add more materials as the week continues. The children may do this activity in a small group or independently.

Materials
recyclable and non-recyclable materials
4 large cardboard boxes

Preparation
Set out three cardboard boxes. Place recyclable and non-recyclable materials in a fourth box.

Variation
Whenever possible, encourage the children to reuse paper in the art center.

Skills Used
Social-Emotional Skills
Critical Thinking Skills

TOWER POWER

Responsibilities
only up to your shoulders.
you have enough room
and your friends.
back in their spaces
finished.

At circle time, discuss block center responsibilities with the children. Reinforce the responsibilities by demonstrating why they are important (example, taller towers built close together are more likely to topple and hurt the children).

Have the children give some examples of different tall buildings they can design. Have small groups of children go into the block area and build a variety of structures. Encourage the children to build with enough space between them so they don't crowd each other. When they are done building, encourage them to place the materials back in their designated area.

Materials
copy of block center responsibilities (below)
unit blocks

Preparation
Make a copy of the block center responsibilities and hang it in the block area.

Block Center Responsibilities
1. Build towers only up to your shoulders.
2. Make sure you have enough room between you and your friends.
3. Place all materials back in their spaces when you have finished.

Variation
Post copies of appropriate rules in each center. Be sure to state them positively, and only have three to four rules in each area.

Skills Used
Social-Emotional Skills
Creative Thinking Skills

BOOK FUN BAG

At circle time, show the children the wonderful books inside the bag (see below). Explain to them that they can take turns taking the tote bag full of books home. Discuss with the children how they are responsible for taking care of the books and returning them to school when they are due back.

Talk about the responsibilities of borrowing books. Show the children how to turn pages slowly so they don't tear. Tell them that books and food or drinks should not be handled at the same time. Share any other rules or ideas you may have. Encourage the children to ask their parents to read to them each day.

Materials
canvas tote bag, two storybooks, photocopies of the parent letter on page 93

Variation
Make Art Fun Bags instead of Book Fun Bags.

Preparation
Place two books in a tote bag and make a copy of the parent letter on page 93. You may want to prepare several tote bags so at least three children can take home a Book Fun Bag each day.

Skills Used
Social-Emotional Skills
Critical Thinking Skills

PARENT LETTER

Date: _____

Dear Parents,

Your child has borrowed one of our Book Fun Bags. Inside the bag, you will find two wonderful children's books. The names of the books are _____ and _____. Please take the time to read and discuss the stories with your child.

The Book Fun Bag activity has three goals. The first is to teach children how to be responsible for materials that they bring home. The second is to encourage reading. The third is to teach children the value of books.

We hope you enjoy this activity and the opportunity it provides for you to spend some quality time with your child. Thank you for your support.

This Book Fun Bag is due back to school on

_____.

Happy Reading!

Sincerely,

LITTER HUNT

Put on a puppet show for the children. Have the puppets talk about litter and let them demonstrate how to pick up litter and throw it in a garbage can. Give each child a sack and have the children go out to the play yard and pick up all the trash they see. When everyone has finished, sit down together and talk about what everyone picked up during the litter hunt. You may want to let the children show each other the pieces of litter they found.

Discuss the great feeling of being responsible by cleaning up litter. Ask the children if they have more ideas about how to keep the planet clean.

Materials
puppets
pieces of litter
paper sacks

Preparation
Prepare a puppet show about litter and how the children can help keep the planet clean. If your play yard is clean, place several pieces of litter around the area.

Variation
Have a neighborhood beautification day and clean up the surrounding areas of your community with families and children.

Skills Used
Motor Skills
Critical Thinking Skills

EVERYBODY CLEAN UP

During circle time, talk to your children about their classroom and how it is their important responsibility to keep it clean. Let the children tell you what they do at home to help keep their house clean. After the discussion, talk to them about the different areas in the classroom that need to be kept clean. Have the children identify some of the areas that they think need a good cleaning. Discuss the concept of teamwork and how working together is faster and can be a lot more fun than working alone.

Divide the children into teams of three. Give each group a broom, a dustpan, and several moist paper towels. Next, have each group select an area in the classroom and begin cleaning. Sing the song "Time to Clean Up" (below) while the children are cleaning up.

Materials

paper towels   brooms

dustpans   trash can

Preparation

Moisten several paper towels. Collect three or four brooms and dustpans. Have an empty trash can nearby.

TIME TO CLEAN UP
Sung to: "The Farmer in the Dell"

It's time to clean up,
It's time to clean up.
Let's work together, now,
It's time to clean up.

Everybody helps,
Everybody helps.
It's time to tidy up our room.
So everybody helps.

Kathleen Cubley

Skills Used
Social-Emotional Skills
Motor Skills

COOPERATION

COOPERATION

The activities in this chapter promote cooperation through a hands-on approach that enables children to cooperate with each other. *Cooperation* means *working together towards a common goal.* It involves getting along with others, using each other's ideas, and working together to accomplish a task. Cooperation is teamwork!

Teaching young children how to cooperate is best done through teacher-child modeling, classroom activities, and taking advantage of opportunities that arise throughout each day. Cooperation can happen at school in many places—in the classroom, on the playground, and in the lunchroom. It is something that should be promoted in every area in the curriculum.

Providing children with the tools to help them learn to cooperate and interact with each other appropriately teaches them a skill that will help them throughout their lives.

TIPS FOR TEACHING COOPERATION

Cooperation is so valuable every day for everyone. You can help children learn to cooperate by keeping the tips below in mind.

- Group activities are a wonderful way to teach cooperation. For example, give each child an art material, and let the children create an art project using each material. You could also have the children work together to use their bodies to form an alphabet letter or a shape.

- Always let children know when you see them cooperating. Take notice when children aren't cooperating, too, and ask them how they could be working together.

- Encourage cooperation by fostering problem-solving skills. When a child notices a problem, have the children work together to come up with possible solutions. Then let them continue to cooperate by putting the solutions into action.

- Cooperation can also be used to manage your learning centers. By allowing only so many children in each center, the children must cooperate in order to keep the right number of children in each area.

- Almost any cooking activity is an excellent method for teaching cooperation.

PIÑATA FUN

Discuss with the children the meaning of the word piñata. Tell them that piñata is a Spanish word, and that Hispanic children use piñatas during celebrations. Divide the children into groups of four. Have the children in each group put on their smocks and go to the art table. Emphasize to the children that they will have to work together to make a piñata. Let them know that it takes more than one child to make a piñata. Demonstrate how to put the glue on the newspaper strips and then place them gently on the balloon. Have the children work together to cover the balloon. Let the balloon dry and continue the project throughout the week.

When you have determined that there is enough paper on the piñata and it is completely dry, set it out for the children to paint and decorate. When the piñata is completely dry, poke the balloon with a needle and let the children take turns pulling the popped balloon out of the shell. Fill each group's piñata with candy and small prizes. Let the children take turns trying to break the piñata.

Materials

balloons
newspaper
scissors
glue
paintbrushes
smocks
paint
bowls

Preparation

Blow up enough balloons so that each group of children can work together on one large balloon. Cover a table with newspaper. Place a medium amount of glue into bowls (two bowls for each group would encourage cooperation). Cut newspaper into strips. Place paper strips and paintbrushes out at the table for the children to use.

Skills Used
Social-Emotional Skills
Creative Thinking Skills

QUESTION, QUESTION

Divide the children into two groups. Have each group make up a team name. Tell the children that you are going to ask each group a question (see below). Anyone in the group can call out the answer. If a group answers correctly, it gets one point. (Use bear counters as point keepers). If a group answers incorrectly, the other group gets to try and answer that question. If that group answers correctly, it gets another turn. If the group doesn't know the answer, the other group gets another turn.

As the game progresses, let the children take turns counting the number of points their group has. This reinforces math and the concept of "points." Continue the game until one of the groups gets seven points.

Materials
bear counters

pen

paper

Variation
Have the questions relate to what the children are studying.

Preparation
Gather materials and write down questions such as these: "What is the name of your school? What is the name of your teacher? Where does Mickey Mouse live? How many fingers do you have on one hand? What color is the grass?"

Skills Used
Social-Emotional Skills
Critical Thinking Skills

TEAM TUGS

Divide the children into groups of four to six. Have each group come up with a team name. Print each team's name on a separate sheet of paper. Encourage each team to decorate its team sign.

Call on two teams. Have one team on one side of the Hula-Hoop (see below) and the other team on the other side of the Hula-Hoop. Let each team grab an end of the rope and hold on as if playing Tug-of-War. The object of the game is to try to pull each other into the hoop. Whichever team doesn't go into the hoop gets to play against a new team. Continue playing until all teams have played. Lead a discussion about teamwork.

Materials

Hula-Hoop   long rope

pen   crayons

paper

Preparation

Find a clean, soft area on the playground. Place a Hula-Hoop in the center of the area and lay the rope next to the hoop.

Variation

Play cooperative games with the children such as The Farmer in the Dell or Duck, Duck, Goose.

Skills Used
Social–Emotional Skills
Creative Thinking Skills

SANDBOX SCULPTING

Show the children pictures of sandcastles and tell them stories about castles. Encourage the children to tell you about castles and how they would build wonderful sandcastles. Show the children the different sand tools and see if they can name the tools. Encourage the children to work cooperatively and build sandcastles together. Take pictures of them building sandcastles, and if you can, play some music while they build their castles. Spend a lot of time on the castles and enjoy the day.

Materials

pictures of sandcastles

buckets

shovels

misting bottles

water

several different shapes and sizes of containers

sandbox

books about castles

Preparation

Set the materials listed above next to a sandbox. Place a couple of large buckets of water at each corner of the sandbox.

Variation

Build a sand town with cars, houses, people, and other buildings.

Skills Used
Social-Emotional Skills
Creative Thinking Skills
Critical Thinking Skills

LEMONADE GANG

Talk to the children about setting up a lemonade stand where they can serve lemonade to their friends. Divide the children into groups. Encourage each group to make a sign for its stand. On each day, a different group of children should prepare the lemonade.

Have the children in one group wash their hands and then sit at the table. Give each child a lemon. Show the children how to roll the lemons back and forth and squish them in their hands. Next, use the sharp knife to cut the lemons in half for each child. Let them squeeze the lemon juice into their paper cups and then put two spoonfuls of sugar into the lemon juice. Have the children stir their juice and sugar and then pour it into the cooperative plastic container. Next, have each child fill a cup with water and add it to the cooperative container. Children take turns stirring with the wooden spoon. Place the lemonade in the refrigerator.

When the lemonade is chilled, have the children set up their lemonade stand and serve lemonade to their friends.

Materials
lemons

water

plastic containers

sugar

spoons

napkins

posterboard

markers

wooden spoon

paper cups

sharp knife for the teacher to use

Preparation
Wash several lemons. Set out a small container of sugar with a few spoons in it and a large plastic container for each group. Have paper cups available. Place posterboard and markers out on a table the children can use to make signs.

Variation
Make different types of lemonade, such as grape juice lemonade, cherry lemonade, or raspberry lemonade.

Skills Used
Motor Skills
Social-Emotional Skills
Critical Thinking Skills

RHYTHM BAND FUN

Set the rhythm instruments out (see below) and introduce them to the children. Let them know that playing in a band takes cooperation and teamwork. Have each child select an instrument. Show the children how to play the instruments and let them practice. Let the children know that when you hold up the instrument card (see below), they are to play that instrument if they have it in their hand.

Have the children play their instruments softly and then a bit louder. Hold up two or three instrument cards at one time. When you take the instrument cards down, the children should stop playing. Use a variety of different cards and let the children switch instruments. Try holding up all of the instrument cards at once.

Materials

rhythm sticks, cymbals, maracas, tambourines, drums, and triangles with strikers; a copy of the instrument cards on page 106; index cards; clear, self-stick paper

Preparation

Photocopy the instrument pictures on page 106. Cut along the lines to make cards. Attach the pictures to index cards and cover them with clear, self-stick paper.

Variation

Have the children march or put on a rhythm band show for their families or other class groups.

Skills Used
Social-Emotional Skills
Creative Thinking Skills

INSTRUMENT CARDS

PEACE CHAIN

Discuss the word peace and how it takes cooperation to spread peace around. Let the children get into different groups and give each group a set of materials (see below). Show them how to glue the strips together to make circles and how to glue the circles together to make chains. Encourage the children to put all their chains together into one long chain—a Peace Chain. As they work together, ask the children what they can do to spread peace around.

Talk about being kind to each other, saying nice things to each other, treating animals kindly, etc.

Materials

scissors
colored construction paper
bottles of glue

Preparation

Cut construction paper into 5-by-1-inch strips. Place the strips in the art area along with bottles of glue.

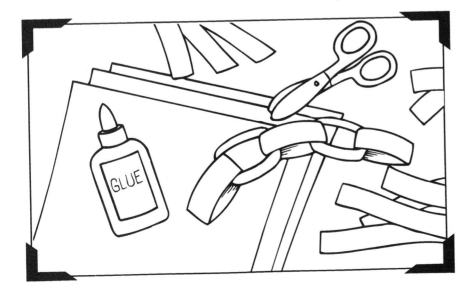

Skills Used
Social-Emotional Skills
Critical Thinking Skills

CONSTRUCTION CITY

Have the children work in cooperative groups. Have the children put on their smocks and begin to create a cooperative community. Give each group a large box to construct a building that will be part of the city. Encourage them to look at pictures of buildings, real or pretend, and observe the different parts of the buildings, such as windows, doors, chimneys, and building materials. Let the children paint their buildings, glue on paper windows, bricks, or whatever creations they can come up with. When the glue and paint are dry, encourage the children to put the community together and play with other props to turn it into a functioning city.

Materials

paint	paintbrushes
paper	child-size scissors
glue	newspaper
smocks	large cardboard boxes

Variation

Let the children make a miniature community with shoeboxes and other small boxes, along with props such as boats, cars, and people.

Preparation

Set out paint, paintbrushes, paper, glue, smocks, glue, and child-size scissors. Set out cardboard boxes in different areas of the classroom or outside. Place newspaper under the boxes.

Skills Used
Social-Emotional Skills
Creative Thinking Skills
Motor Skills
Creative Thinking Skills

FLYING THE FRIENDLY SKIES

Have each child select a colored pipe cleaner and twist it onto his or her wrist to make a wristband. Have the children find others with the same colored wristbands and form a team. Have each team think of a name. Let each team pretend to be airplanes and take turns putting on an air show. Encourage them to fly in circles and free form. When all the teams have had a turn demonstrating their flying skills, call out a color and have that team fly until you call out a different color.

Materials
different colors of pipe cleaners, three or four per color

Preparation
Place the pipe cleaners out so the children can see the different colors.

Variation
Play music and let the children dance in their groups.

Skills Used
Social-Emotional Skills
Creative Thinking Skills
Motor Skills
Creative Thinking Skills

PARACHUTE FUN

Have a group of ten children or more circle around a parachute, hold onto the edge, and lift the parachute. Let them see how important it is for everyone to work together. Show them that if they don't work together, the parachute won't go up or move the way they want it to. Have everyone lift the parachute up and then down, go under the parachute, and come out of the parachute. Have the children continue to hold onto the parachute and go clockwise and then counterclockwise. Repeat the directions and encourage everyone to cooperate and work together.

Materials
parachute

Preparation
Set out the parachute.

Variation
Toss balls onto the parachute and encourage the children to keep the balls bouncing.

Skills Used
Motor Skills
Social-Emotional Skills

ART MURAL

Explain to the children what a mural is. Talk about some of the murals in your town that they might have seen. Show them pictures of murals in an art book. Divide the children into groups of four. Encourage each group to decide on a mural topic. Ideas include flowers, animals, their classroom, a zoo, an ocean scene, and so on. Also let them know that as a group, they can choose to swirl paint or mix colors and create an abstract mural.

Turn the music on and let the children create their cooperative murals. When they have finished and the paint is dry, let them print their names in the corner of the paper. Let the children tell their classmates about their murals. Hang the murals for all the children and parents to see.

Materials

scissors
butcher paper
tape player or radio
classical, jazz, or children's
　　music
paint
paintbrushes
plastic paint containers
markers
art books
smocks

Preparation

Cut a long sheet of butcher paper for each group. Place the paper in areas where the different groups can paint their murals. Lay enough smocks next to each piece of paper, and put paintbrushes and paint out.

Variation

Use another art medium, such as clay, to do group sculpting.

Skills Used
Creative Thinking Skills
Motor Skills

STORYTELLING

Talk to the children about storytelling. Pick a topic and start to tell a story. Encourage the children to add to the story as it unravels. You can have them make sound effects, dramatize the story, sing about the story, or make up a finger play about the story.

Put the children in situations in which they must cooperate to get out of a problem. You might try naming four or five children, and then tell them that they are up in a tall tree. Have them tell a story about what to do to get out of the tree. Facilitate a cooperative story and solution. Other ideas for cooperative stories include fixing a broken playground toy, building a house, and playing a game.

Telling stories with children can also help them deal with situations such as getting along with each other, racial problems, and emotions. Letting the children take turns telling the story and cooperating in the story is a great outlet and encourages cooperative listening and cooperative storytelling.

Materials
blanket

Variation
Tell group stories using props, or write stories together.

Preparation
Spread a blanket out on the floor indoors or in a shady outdoor area.

Skills Used
Social-Emotional Skills
Critical Thinking Skills

BEAD NECKLACES

In small groups, have the children create beads out of the clay (see below). Encourage them to mix the colors together and share ideas. Show them how to put a hole in the beads they make by sticking a toothpick through the bead and rolling it on the table. As the children create the beads, have them place the beads in the center of the work area on the paper plate. Let the children make many different beads.

Bake the beads according to the package directions. When the beads are ready, set them out on a table along with pieces of string and needles. Let the children choose several beads. Encourage the children to cooperate and help make sure they each have the same amount of beads. Help the children string the beads to make necklaces. Invite them to admire the different beads that they chose to make their necklaces.

Materials
knife for the teacher to use, a variety of colored Fimo clay, toothpicks, paper plates, string, needles

Preparation
Cut the Fimo clay into ¼-inch cubes. Set out the different colors on a table. Set out toothpicks and a paper plate. Cut string into 12" lengths.

Variation
Create bead bracelets.

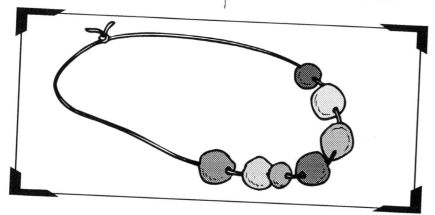

Skills Used
Social-Emotional Skills
Creative Thinking Skills
Motor Skills

ICE CREATIONS

Have a small group of children put on their smocks. Let the children go to the different buckets (see below). Let each child pick a few plastic containers. Children can fill their containers with the colored water. Place the containers in the freezer. Let the other groups have a chance to do the same process.

The following day, divide the children into cooperative groups. Give each group a variety of frozen containers and let the children push the ice out of the containers. Have each group create an ice creation by placing the different shapes of ice in formations. Let the children sprinkle a little salt over the areas where they want ice pieces to stick together.

Encourage each group to give its ice creation a name. Let the children take turns telling each group about their creation.

Materials

small buckets

food coloring

plastic cups

wooden spoons

smocks

empty frozen juice cans

small plastic containers of various sizes that the children can pour water into and freeze

salt

Preparation

Fill each bucket with water. Stir a few drops of food coloring into each bucket to make a variety of different colors. Set the buckets outside along with the other materials. Place a few plastic cups in each bucket and set different containers next to each bucket.

Variation

Purchase bags of ice cubes and let each group create an ice castle or any creation it desires.

Skills Used
Critical Skills
Creative Thinking Skills
Motor Skills

WATER PLAY SHOW

Select six children to put on a water show for the other children. Show the children how to operate spray bottles to make different misting and squirting techniques. Play some music and let the children squirt water to the rhythm. Be sure to set some rules for the children to follow, such as no squirting each other or you!

Let all the other children sit down and watch as the six children present a cooperative water play show. Let all the children take turns working in small groups. You may want to do a group each day so the children can have time to plan and practice their show.

Materials

six spray bottles   music

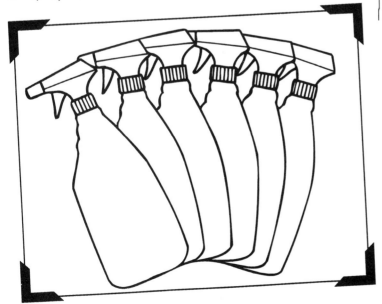

Preparation

Fill the spray bottles with water and set them out in a grassy area.

Variation

Have small groups of children put on dance shows.

Skills Used
Motor Skills
Social-Emotional Skills
Creative Thinking Skills

HOKEY POKEY

Have the children gather in a large circle. Sing the song, "Hokey Pokey," with the children and encourage them to do the movements as described. This activity teaches cooperation because it takes teamwork to follow the directions and cooperate in a community sense.

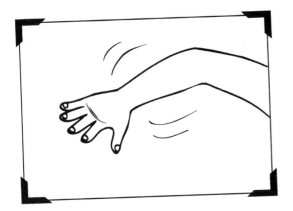

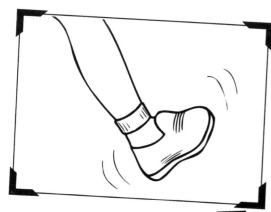

HOKEY POKEY

You put your right arm in,
You put your right arm out,
You put your right arm in, and you shake it all about.
You do the Hokey Pokey, and you turn yourself around,
That's what it's all about.

You put your left arm in,
You put your left arm out,
You put your left arm in, and you shake it all about.
You do the Hokey Pokey, and you turn yourself around,
That's what it's all about.

You put your right foot in,
You put your right foot out,
You put your right foot in, and you shake it all about.
You do the Hokey Pokey, and you turn yourself around,
That's what it's all about.

You put your left foot in,
You put your left foot out,
You put your left foot in, and you shake it all about.
You do the Hokey Pokey, and you turn yourself around,
That's what it's all about.

You put your head in,
You put your head out,
You put your head in, and you shake it all about.
You do the Hokey Pokey, and you turn yourself around,
That's what it's all about.

Traditional

Materials
none

Preparation
none

Variation
Play Duck, Duck, Goose.

Skills Used
Social-Emotional Skills
Motor Skills

THIS IS THE WAY WE WASH OUR CLOTHES

Have groups of three children fill buckets of water to empty into the wash tub. Have them determine how much soap they should add to the water. Explain to them that they will have the opportunity to wash their dolls' clothes today. Explain that in the olden days, people didn't have washers and dryers. Let them know that clothes were washed by hand. Show them how to swish the clothing in the wash water, ring it dry, and hang it on the clothesline to dry.

The children will have to share the clothing. They may choose to form an assembly line, where one child washes the clothes, another wrings them out, and another hangs them on the clothesline. When the clothes are dried, the children are responsible for taking the clothing down and returning it to the basket.

Materials

clothesline

clothespins

large wash tub

soap

buckets

laundry basket

doll clothes

Preparation

Set up a clothesline. Set out clothespins, a wash tub, soap, buckets, and a laundry basket.

Variation

Let the children wash and dry dishes together.

Skills Used

Social-Emotional Skills

Motor Skills

PIONEER CAMP

Read a story to the children about pioneer life. Talk about how pioneers lived and about all the different tools they used. Show the children the prop boxes (see below). Explain to them that they will work together to set up a pioneer camp. They will first make their house out of the boxes, sheets, rope, and clothespins. They can use the other props to decorate and live in their camp home.

As the children work together constructing their camp home, give them guidance when necessary. You might help them construct their tents, for example, or provide other materials they may request. Encourage their creativity.

Materials

old sheets

large and small cardboard boxes

clothespins

rope

dishes

a wide variety of other props that would enhance pioneer camp

books about pioneer days

Preparation

Depending on the amount of materials you have available, make one or more prop boxes. Each prop box should contain the following: sheet, boxes, clothespins, rope, dishes, candles, and pioneer clothing, such as boots, hats, and suspenders. Set the prop boxes outside or inside in a place that will allow the children to have plenty of room to set up camp.

Skills Used
Social-Emotional Skills
Motor Skills
Critical Thinking Skills
Creative Thinking Skills

MOVE TO THE MUSIC

Let the children listen to the music. Encourage them to hold hands and move together in a large group. They can go around in circles, hold hands, and move together into the middle of the circle and then back again making a large circle. The children can also have a smaller circle inside a larger circle. Everyone can hold hands and go up and down with their legs, bend forward and backward, etc. Spend time playing different types of music.

Take breaks and enjoy food and conversation. Have fun with music and movement. The children can do cooperative group dances such as the bump, the electric slide, etc. You can teach them dances such as the swim, the monkey, and the twist. Teach the children to enjoy music and dance.

Materials

music   lemonade
cups   pretzels
napkins

Preparation

Set up music and food.

Variation

Focus on specific types of music so the children are able to identify jazz, classical music, modern music, etc.

Skills Used
Social-Emotional Skills
Motor Skills

CLOUD WATCH

Take the children outside and have them lay on the ground and look up at the sky. Talk about the clouds in the sky. Ask the children what the clouds look like and have them describe the different shapes, colors, and textures of the clouds. Ask the children what it would be like to travel up to the clouds and live on a cloud. You can tell cloud stories, recite cloud rhymes, and make up cloud songs.

After observing the clouds, tell a cooperative story such as the following: One fine sunny day, the children were laying around watching the clouds go by. All of a sudden, a big wind came and blew the children high into the sky. They all landed on a big cloud and had to work together to figure out a way to get off the cloud.

Have the children help think about how they can get off the cloud. Let the children take turns finishing the story.

Materials

blanket or just a warm grassy area large enough to accommodate all the children in the group, cloudy day with partial blue skies

Variation

Do the same activity, but use trees instead of clouds.

Preparation

Skills Used
Creative Thinking Skills
Critical Thinking Skills

FEED THE BIRDS

Discuss wild birds with the children. Let them look at the pictures in the books. Take the children outside and look for birds in trees, bushes, and other places. See if the children can identify any of the birds.

Back inside, let the children make bird feeders. Have them spread suet onto pine cones and roll them in birdseed. Have the children walk outside together and determine where to place their feeders. Encourage the children to sit together and watch birds.

Materials

scissors

yarn

a pine cone for each child

suet

spoons

birdseed

newspaper

books about birds

Preparation

Cut six-inch strands of yarn for each pine cone. Tie the yarn onto the top of each pine cone. Place newspaper out on a table. Set out suet and plastic spoons, and set birdseed out on newspaper.

Variation

Put up a variety of bird feeders and birdbaths. Have the children take turns filling the feeders and the bath.

Skills Used
Motor Skills
Critical Thinking Skills

SHAPEY THE ROBOT

Introduce the children to Shapey the Robot. Tell the children a story about how Shapey lost all of its shapes and parts. Shapey needs eyes, ears, a nose, a mouth, hands, and legs. Have the children work together to put Shapey back together.

Divide the children into groups of two or three. Give each group the materials needed for the project. Encourage the groups to talk about how they want to put their robot together. When the robots are finished, let each group introduce its robot to the rest of the groups.

Materials

scissors, construction paper, glue, variety of boxes, craft sticks, old knobs, nuts and bolts, etc.

Preparation

Cut out a variety of different shapes for the children to glue onto the boxes. Set out all of the materials the children can put on their boxes. Set out glue, shapes, paper, and scissors.

Variation

Create a rainbow robot using paint, paper, and other colorful items.

Skills Used
Social-Emotional Skills
Critical Thinking Skills

PHOTO ALBUMS

Divide children into groups of four. Have each of the four children select one piece of paper. This will be a photo album page. Let each child select two or three photographs (see below) to glue onto his or her piece of paper. Encourage them to decorate the pages with stickers and different designs. Help the children print the names of the children in the pictures.

Have the group create an album cover. They can work together selecting stickers and making designs. Put the album together with brads or yarn, and place it in the language arts center for the children to look through during the year. The children can add to it or make additional albums.

Materials

construction paper
glue sticks or glue
stickers
brads or yarn

hole punch
photos of children
markers

Preparation

Punch holes in six pieces of construction paper. Set out paper and other materials.

Variation

Have the children's parents bring in family pictures to create a school family album.

Skills Used
Creative Thinking Skills
Social-Emotional Skills

VISION BOXES

Divide the children into groups of three or four. Give each group a shoebox, a pile of pictures, and glue. Let each group of children look through its pictures and decide on a theme. Have them glue the pictures to the box. Encourage them to cover the tops and all sides of their boxes.

Let the boxes dry. Cut a small hole in the top of the boxes, big enough for a child's hand to fit in. Before circle time, place objects inside the boxes that correlate with the pictures on the outside of the box. For example, if the children have glued pictures of leaves on the box, put a leaf or twig inside the box.

During circle time, talk about how the children worked together creating the vision boxes. Then let some of the children have a turn placing their hand in a box and pulling out an object. Next, let the children find the picture on the box that correlates with the object. Let other children take turns. These vision boxes can be used over and over again at circle time to encourage language, cooperation, and sensory skills.

Materials

scissors, magazines, glue, shoeboxes

Variation

Use different textures of paper. See if the children can feel the different textures and match each texture on the box to the actual textured paper in the box.

Preparation

Cut out interesting pictures from different magazines. Set out pictures, glue, scissors, and shoeboxes in a central location in the classroom.

Skills Used
Creative Thinking Skills
Motor Skills
Critical Thinking Skills

FRUITY FUN MIX

Divide the children into groups of four or five. Have the children in one group wash their hands and then go to the station (see below). Explain to them that they are in charge of making a snack for the class. They will fill the bags with a spoonful of each ingredient. (It is best to have one ingredient for each child at the station.) Have the first child take a bag and put in a spoonful of raisins. Then the child passes the bag to the next child who puts in another ingredient, and so on. The child to put in the last ingredient should also seal the bag and put it into the collection basket or box.

Materials

large box of raisins, yogurt covered raisins, dried pineapple, sunflower seeds, diced dates, dried apples or other dried fruits; six teaspoons; six plastic or paper bowls; a snack-size resealable plastic bag for each child; large bag or basket; spoons

Preparation

Cut any of the dried fruit that is not bite-size into bite-size pieces. Place each ingredient in a separate bowl, along with a spoon. Set these out with the resealable bags.

Variation

Have the children take turns making class snacks by changing ingredients.

Skills Used
Motor Skills
Social-Emotional Skills

Totline® PUBLICATIONS

THEME CALENDARS
Activities for every day.
Toddler Theme Calendar
Preschool Theme Calendar
Kindergarten Theme Calendar

TIME TO LEARN
Ideas for hands-on learning.
Colors • Letters • Measuring •
Numbers • Science • Shapes •
Matching and Sorting • New Words
• Cutting and Pasting •
Drawing and Writing • Listening •
Taking Care of Myself

Teacher Resources

ART SERIES
Ideas for successful art experiences.
Cooperative Art
Special Day Art
Outdoor Art

BEST OF TOTLINE® SERIES
Totline's best ideas.
Best of Totline Newsletter
Best of Totline Bear Hugs
Best of Totline Parent Flyers

BUSY BEES SERIES
Seasonal ideas for twos and threes.
Fall • Winter • Spring • Summer

CELEBRATIONS SERIES
Early learning through celebrations.
Small World Celebrations
Special Day Celebrations
Great Big Holiday Celebrations
Celebrating Likes and Differences

CIRCLE TIME SERIES
Put the spotlight on circle time!
Introducing Concepts at Circle Time
Music and Dramatics at Circle Time
Storytime Ideas for Circle Time

EMPOWERING KIDS SERIES
Positive solutions to behavior issues.
Can-Do Kids
Problem-Solving Kids

EXPLORING SERIES
Versatile, hands-on learning.
Exploring Sand • Exploring Water

FOUR SEASONS
Active learning through the year.
Art • Math • Movement • Science

JUST RIGHT PATTERNS
8-page, reproducible pattern folders.
Valentine's Day • St. Patrick's Day •
Easter • Halloween • Thanksgiving •
Hanukkah • Christmas • Kwanzaa •
Spring • Summer • Autumn •
Winter • Air Transportation • Land
Transportation • Service Vehicles
• Water Transportation • Train
• Desert Life • Farm Life • Forest
Life • Ocean Life • Wetland Life
• Zoo Life • Prehistoric Life

KINDERSTATION SERIES
Learning centers for kindergarten.
Calculation Station
Communication Station
Creation Station
Investigation Station

1•2•3 SERIES
Open-ended learning.
Art • Blocks • Games • Colors •
Puppets • Reading & Writing •
Math • Science • Shapes

1001 SERIES
Super reference books.
1001 Teaching Props
1001 Teaching Tips
1001 Rhymes & Fingerplays

PIGGYBACK® SONG BOOKS
New lyrics sung to favorite tunes!
Piggyback Songs
More Piggyback Songs
Piggyback Songs for Infants
and Toddlers
Holiday Piggyback Songs
Animal Piggyback Songs
Piggyback Songs for School
Piggyback Songs to Sign
Spanish Piggyback Songs
More Piggyback Songs for School

PROJECT BOOK SERIES
*Reproducible, cross-curricular project
books and project ideas.*
Start With Art
Start With Science

REPRODUCIBLE RHYMES
*Make-and-take-home books for
emergent readers.*
Alphabet Rhymes • Object Rhymes

SNACKS SERIES
Nutrition combines with learning.
Super Snacks • Healthy Snacks •
Teaching Snacks • Multicultural Snacks

TERRIFIC TIPS
Handy resources with valuable ideas.
Terrific Tips for Directors
Terrific Tips for Toddler Teachers
Terrific Tips for Preschool Teachers

THEME-A-SAURUS® SERIES
Classroom-tested, instant themes.
Theme-A-Saurus
Theme-A-Saurus II
Toddler Theme-A-Saurus
Alphabet Theme-A-Saurus
Nursery Rhyme Theme-A-Saurus
Storytime Theme-A-Saurus
Multisensory Theme-A-Saurus
Transportation Theme-A-Saurus
Field Trip Theme-A-Saurus

TODDLER RESOURCES
Great for working with 18 mos–3 yrs.
Playtime Props for Toddlers
Toddler Art

Parent Resources

A YEAR OF FUN SERIES
Age-specific books for parenting.
Just for Babies • Just for Ones •
Just for Twos • Just for Threes •
Just for Fours • Just for Fives

LEARN WITH PIGGYBACK® SONGS
*Captivating music with
age-appropriate themes.*
Songs & Games for…
Babies • Toddlers • Threes • Fours
Sing a Song of…
Letters • Animals • Colors • Holidays
• Me • Nature • Numbers

LEARN WITH STICKERS
*Beginning workbook and first reader
with 100-plus stickers.*
Balloons • Birds • Bows • Bugs •
Butterflies • Buttons • Eggs • Flags •
Flowers • Hearts • Leaves • Mittens

MY FIRST COLORING BOOK
*White illustrations on black back-
grounds—perfect for toddlers!*
All About Colors
All About Numbers
Under the Sea
Over and Under
Party Animals
Tops and Bottoms

PLAY AND LEARN
Activities for learning through play.
Blocks • Instruments • Kitchen
Gadgets • Paper • Puppets • Puzzles

RAINY DAY FUN
*This activity book for parent-child fun
keeps minds active on rainy days!*

RHYME & REASON STICKER WORKBOOKS
*Sticker fun to boost
language development and
thinking skills.*
Up in Space
All About Weather
At the Zoo
On the Farm
Things That Go
Under the Sea

SEEDS FOR SUCCESS
*Ideas to help children develop
essential life skills for future success.*
Growing Creative Kids
Growing Happy Kids
Growing Responsible Kids
Growing Thinking Kids

Posters
Celebrating Childhood Posters
Reminder Posters

Puppet Pals
Instant puppets!
Children's Favorites • The Three Bears
• Nursery Rhymes • Old MacDonald
• More Nursery Rhymes • Three
Little Pigs • Three Billy Goats Gruff •
Little Red Riding Hood

Manipulatives
CIRCLE PUZZLES
African Adventure Puzzle

LITTLE BUILDER STACKING CARDS
Castle • The Three Little Pigs

Tot-Mobiles
*Each set includes four punch-out,
easy-to-assemble mobiles.*
Animals & Toys
Beginning Concepts
Four Seasons

Start right, start bright!

NEW!
Early Learning Resources

For Teachers

Art Series

Great ideas for exploring art with children ages 3 to 6! Easy, inexpensive activities encourage enjoyable art experiences in a variety of ways.

Cooperative Art • Outdoor Art • Special Day Art

The Best of Totline—Bear Hugs

This new resource is a collection of some of Totline's best ideas for fostering positive behavior.

Celebrating Childhood Posters

Inspire parents, staff, and yourself with these endearing posters with poems by Jean Warren.

The Children's Song
Patterns
Pretending
Snowflake Splendor
The Heart of a Child
Live Like the Child
The Light of Childhood
A Balloon
The Gift of Rhyme

Circle Time Series

Teachers will discover quick, easy ideas to incorporate into their lessons when they gather children together for this important time of the day.

Introducing Concepts at Circle Time
Music and Dramatics at Circle Time
Storytime Ideas for Circle Time

Empowering Kids

This unique series tackles behavioral issues in typical Totline fashion—practical ideas for empowering young children with self-esteem and basic social skills.

Problem-Solving Kids
Can-Do Kids

Theme-A-Saurus

Two new theme books join this popular Totline series!

Transportation Theme-A-Saurus
Field Trip Theme-A-Saurus

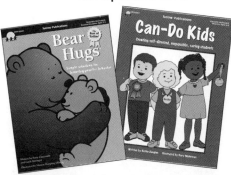

For Parents

My First Coloring Book Series

These coloring books are truly appropriate for toddlers—black backgrounds with white illustrations. That means no lines to cross and no-lose coloring fun! Bonus stickers included!

All About Colors
All About Numbers
Under the Sea
Over and Under
Party Animals
Tops and Bottoms

Happy Days

Seasonal fun with rhymes and songs, snack recipes, games, and arts and crafts.

Pumpkin Days • Turkey Days • Holly Days • Snowy Days

Little Builder Stacking Cards

Each game box includes 48 unique cards with different scenes printed on each side. Children can combine the cards that bend in the middle with the flat cards to form simple buildings or tall towers!

Castle
The Three Little Pigs

Rainy Day Fun

Turn rainy-day blahs into creative, learning fun! These creative Totline ideas turn a home into a jungle, post office, grocery store, and more!

Rhyme & Reason Sticker Workbooks

These age-appropriate workbooks combine language and thinking skills for a guaranteed fun learning experience. More than 100 stickers!

Up in Space • All About Weather • At the Zoo • On the Farm • Things That Go • Under the Sea

Theme Calendars

Weekly activity ideas in a nondated calendar for exploring the seasons with young children.

Toddler Theme Calendar
Preschool Theme Calendar
Kindergarten Theme Calendar

Totline products are available at fine parent and teacher stores.